MW01671910

2024-2025

TRENDBOOK

National Association
of *Independent* Schools

ISBN: 978-1-63115-055-5
Printed in the United States of America

National Association
of *Independent* Schools

The National Association of Independent Schools provides services to more than 2,000 schools and associations of schools in the United States and abroad, including more than 1,700 nonprofit, private K-12 schools in the U.S. that are self-determining in mission and program and are governed by independent boards. As the largest association of independent schools, NAIS co-creates the future of education by uniting and empowering our community.

For more information, go to the NAIS website at http://www.nais.org.

Editors: Susan Hunt, Myra McGovern, Karla Taylor
Design: Fletcher Design, Inc./Washington, DC
Photography: James Kegley Photography

Table of Contents

A Fresh Look at Today—and Tomorrow

By Debra P. Wilson, NAIS President

This year's edition of the *NAIS Trendbook* is the 15th, a milestone of sorts. And like all milestones, it provides an opportunity to reflect on where we were, where we are, where we're going, and why.

A look back to the first *Trendbook* is a bit of a history lesson. In that edition, chapters focused on then-timely topics ranging from the slow recovery from the Great Recession of 2008 to the emergence of social media (including such new concepts as "tweeting"). The topics I wrote about for that first edition, "The Legislative, Regulatory, and Legal Outlook" and "The Human Resources Outlook," were a little less unique to those times. But they, too, aimed to provide insights into what was happening in the moment and what we thought might be coming around the corner.

That first *Trendbook* was the outcome of an end-of-year senior leadership team meeting at NAIS, when we were all just talking about what we had experienced that year and what we could see happening for independent schools in the year ahead. As he was prone to do, then-President Pat Bassett threw out an idea: He said he wished more school leaders could hear the conversation.

After much scurrying to pull the chapters together, the *Trendbook* was born. We envisioned the *Trendbook* as a way to stimulate broad, community-wide conversation about big issues of the moment, and to encourage data- and research-based decision-making. We hoped schools would use this information as a starting point for the year, to consider their own data, outlook, and experience in the context of these larger trends.

Fifteen years later, the *Trendbook*'s goals remain largely the same. However, when I became president in August 2023, it seemed time to take a fresh look. We wanted to make sure the book is still helping schools meet today's moment—a moment I think you'd agree feels quite different from 2010. For example, many schools now engage in strategic planning and decision-making not just annually but all year long. A potentially hot trend or topic can burn itself out between when a *Trendbook* chapter is written and when we go to the printer. Similarly, asteroid moments seem to appear midyear with alarming regularity.

In revisiting the *Trendbook*, we spent some time talking about these issues and how to ensure that the book continues to be a guiding resource for our member schools. We know that for many schools, it's used to inform board meetings early in the year, and afterward the content continues to provide fodder for strategic conversations at all levels of leadership. For us at NAIS, developing the book is an important cross-collaborative effort that both informs and guides our work each year. Even the exercise of creating it provides a unique moment for reflection and collaboration.

In this *2024-2025 Trendbook* you'll see some differences that grew out of these recent reflections. Most obviously, you'll get an early look at the new NAIS brand we're rolling out at about the same time this book hits desks.

The more substantive change is a broadening of focus. We explore a few topics that play out beyond the walls of our schools but that are likely to shape our future. For example, you'll see chapters addressing topics like changes in higher education and in AI. While some of these topics, or ones related to them, have made brief appearances in previous editions of the *Trendbook*, you will find more depth here. In most chapters you will also see a new feature titled "On the Horizon," which provides some conjecture about what we might see around the next corner. We anticipate that the *Trendbook* topics and format will continue to shift over time as trends change and their varied impacts appear on the horizon.

I believe these changes reflect something important. Independent schools don't exist in a vacuum. While we must attend to our day-to-day issues—and there are many, many issues to tackle in the course of a typical independent school day—we must also keep an eye on the future. I hope that the *Trendbook* will continue to be a tool to help you expand your view in this way. For those of you who have had enough of change and of living in "unprecedented times," the book still includes the data and insights you have come to expect and rely on, as we know that this information remains vital.

I also hope the *Trendbook* will continue to prompt conversation in the independent school community. Whether we gather virtually or in person, and whenever we pick up the phone and reach out to a colleague at another school, it's useful to have shared information that we can reflect on together.

IF WE WERE CELEBRATING a 15th wedding anniversary, we'd be exchanging crystal gifts. While I would love to be able to make crystal ball predictions, alas, those are cloudy as we go to press. In fact, I think you'll agree that the last 15 years have been a reminder that all we can say for sure is this: Change is the only constant.

As a community, however, we can prepare ourselves with information and support each other through challenges as they present themselves. The visuals in our new NAIS brand focus on the letter *I* in the name *NAIS*. This is because we are *independent* schools but also because we are *innovative*, *interdependent*, *inclusive*, *inspiring*, *impactful*, and always *improving*. I look forward to opportunities in the year ahead to share perspectives on how the *Trendbook* forecasts play out in our school communities.

PART 1

This section covers 21 trends shaping the future of independent schools, plus questions, steps, and resources to put ideas into action.

1

The Financial Sustainability Forecast

By Mark J. Mitchell

Mark J. Mitchell is vice president of access and affordability at NAIS.

Key Takeaways

- Independent schools have entered a new era of competition as alternatives, such as charter schools, microschools, and homeschooling, have filled the demand for flexible, values-driven, customer-based choices. High-quality public schools also threaten the demand for independent schools.
- Changing market dynamics and economic volatility will pose ongoing financial and competitive challenges for independent schools, necessitating proactive financial management and enrollment marketing strategies.
- Pursued correctly, new forms of support from alumni and state programs have the potential to play a role in sustaining independent schools.

Increasing Competition from Alternative School Models Will Push Independent Schools to Better Define Their Unique Value

For the typical independent school, the financial stability of its business model is driven by enrollment (the largest revenue generator) and staffing (the largest expense generator). Many other aspects of the financial model also come into play, such as charitable giving, endowment, program, and physical plant. But the forecast for long-term financial stability boils down to this: Schools must be able to sustain or grow enrollment; charge a tuition price that families will accept and that can support a high-value program distinct from other schools; and staff the program to deliver high-quality experiences in the most cost-effective ways. To be sustainable in the years ahead, schools will find it increasingly important to consider the external and internal forces that impact their enrollment, pricing, and staffing.

A major external force affecting enrollment demand is competition—and not just from other independent schools. Several factors shape the competitive challenges independent schools are facing on many fronts.

Price and quality. As tuitions have risen, so too have the wealth profiles that families need to be able to comfortably afford one or two independent school tuitions. But in many markets, independent schools' primary competitors are, increasingly, public or charter schools, which charge no tuition. To heighten the challenge, as families who *can* pay independent school tuitions get wealthier, the likelihood grows that they live in neighborhoods where the public school options appear to be of comparable or even better quality than independent schools.

Unless independent schools have a clear and intentional strategy for creating and communicating their unique value, parent demand may wane in some markets, particularly those where the perceived outcomes for the price push families to look for less expensive options they believe are at least "good enough." Proving that the school's price is worth the cost for full-tuition-paying families will be key to generating tuition revenue that bolsters the school's financial foundation.

Flexibility and personalization. The United States is experiencing notable and continued growth in educational alternatives such as microschools and homeschooling. The National Microschooling Center estimates that some 95,000 microschools served about 1.5 million students in the U.S. in 2023.[1] And nearly 3.7 million children under 18 were homeschooled, according to a U.S. Census Bureau Household Pulse Survey of households conducted in April/May 2024.[2] Among these schools' attractive features are flexibility, accommodation to unique needs, and hyper-attention to each child—all at a fraction of the price of an independent school.

As the proliferation of (and confidence in) these educational alternatives grows, maintaining enrollment—and the financial sustainability—of the independent school option will require more intentional work to show value and differentiation, as well as the ability to adapt in mission-aligned ways to the new demands of the market.

Alignment with families' values. NAIS research about why parents choose independent schools indicates that a top motive is the desire to nurture children's potential in a values-aligned community.[3] The values parents seek vary from family to family, but political, religious, and social values certainly are top of mind for many. In a 2022 study, the National Center for Education Statistics found that when it came to families' reasons for homeschooling their children, 74.7% cited "a desire to provide moral instruction"—slightly more than those who cited "dissatisfaction with academic instruction at other schools" (72.6%). More than half (58.9%) gave as a reason "a desire to provide religious instruction."[4]

In the contentious presidential election year of 2024, political and social polarization may manifest itself in choices parents make about where to educate their children. For instance, some may consider which are the "liberal" or "conservative" schools in their markets and reorient their choices about where to educate their children accordingly.

All these sources of competition point to the need for schools to be intentional about creating and communicating the unique value they offer for the price they are asking. For schools that consider themselves to be the "best-kept secret in town," it will be critical to take strategic and concerted action to be known for higher quality, values-driven, and higher touch experiences compared to the alternatives.

Changing Market Dynamics and Economic Volatility Will Pose Ongoing Competitive and Financial Challenges

In addition to the growing number of schooling choices, two other factors are likely to affect schools' financial sustainability.

The shrinking student pipeline. Demographic change has a tremendous influence on the enrollment stability of independent schools. According to estimates and projections for school-age population by EASI Demographics for the NAIS Demographic Center, the past few years have seen population decline among children in every age group studied. While the projections from 2023 to 2028 forecast upturns in each age group, the growth will be moderate or slow, with under 2% growth projected overall, and the total number will still be less than that of 2020.[5] (See the Demographics section on page 98.) While this national trend will play out differently in different regions, states, and cities, fewer school-age children in the pipeline will heighten the competition for private school enrollment. Even growing numbers of children don't guarantee enrollment success, particularly in an environment where technology and competitive alternatives change how families view the independent school difference. Again, retaining or growing enrollment in an environment of constricted population growth will require strategic and creative approaches to marketing, recruitment, and value creation.

Economic challenges. Inflation and interest rates remain difficult to predict and may continue to create short- and medium-term pressure on school budgets. Lingering higher-than-typical inflation not only affects consumers' confidence in their ability to afford private school costs but also impacts faculty and staff anxiety about their own earnings and the prospect of sufficient salary increases in the school budget. The fight against inflation has also led to higher interest rates and increased borrowing costs, which restrict schools' ability to use resources in strategic ways. Rates are likely to fall: The Federal Reserve Board's "Summary of Economic Projections" for June 2024 suggests that the Federal Reserve could cut the federal funds rate (which drives other rates) in 2024 and through 2026.[6] But the decline will be slow, and refinancing debts will remain less attractive.

A continuing economic challenge is the question of teachers' salaries. As noted in Chapter 2, "The Workforce Forecast," teachers in general—not just at independent schools—make 26.4% less on average than professionals with similar education.[7] See "The Workforce Forecast" for more about teacher satisfaction and retention.

To manage demographics-driven enrollment change amid pressure to increase staff compensation and program enhancements in high-inflation times, schools need financial, operational, and staffing models that can flex as conditions warrant. Today more than ever, it is critical that school leaders have the skills to develop and strategize for realistic three- to five-year budget, enrollment, and scenario plans that leverage creativity in nontuition revenue sources.

Alumni Engagement and Support from States Could Play a Bigger Role in the Future

Fundraising and state government sources are other components of financial sustainability that could grow in importance for schools that prioritize them.

Deepening the donor pool. Charitable gifts have long been a crucial part of a school's financial foundation. Fundraising made up 5.3% of all revenue for day schools in 2023-2024 and 11.8% for boarding schools.[8]

Typically, annual giving campaigns depend heavily on current parents as a (if not *the*) primary donor pool. Many schools have found it difficult to consistently engage a larger, more reliable pool of other supporters. According to NAIS data on annual giving for the 2022-2023 academic year, the median participation rate among alumni was just 8.0%, compared to 65.9% among current parents—a percentage that had itself declined from 67.7% in 2021-2022.[9] As current parents feel increased pressure to be able to pay tuition, their likelihood of continued strong engagement in giving campaigns appears to be weakening.

Strategically engaging alumni in new ways is an area of opportunity for many schools seeking to replace, balance, or supplement parent giving. Understanding what motivates different supporters to sustain their belief in the school's present and future needs requires strategic attention and creative campaigns beyond one-size-fits-all appeals. The effort can pay off in additional ways for schools that pursue major gifts (with or without a capital campaign) and planned gifts. Properly cultivated alumni are a natural source of potential donors who want to help sustain their school now and in future years.

Considering the role of education savings accounts. As Chapter 3, "The Legal and Legislative Forecast," makes clear, financial support for private schools from state governments has grown in recent years. This support can come in different forms, including vouchers and tax credit scholarships. In addition, more and more states are establishing education savings accounts (ESAs), which provide state-funded cash that families can use for private school tuition or other school expenses. ESA amounts are typically based on a percentage of the state's per-pupil education funding and can range from $6,000 to $10,000 a year, depending on the state. Many of these programs have income-based restrictions or are limited to serving certain types of students (such as those with disabilities or attending low-performing schools). But movement toward ESAs with universal eligibility is growing. Nearly 330,000 students in 2023-2024 have received ESA funding, according to EdChoice.[10]

In states where ESA programs are available for families, school leaders may find a new pool of prospective families for whom sticker price is a little less of an issue. Or schools may be able to use ESAs as a new lever to help retain current families by making tuition easier to work into their family budgets.

But as Chapter 3 points out, working with ESAs or other state programs requires careful consideration.

In these markets, schools would be wise to examine whether these funds can help expand enrollment or whether they are used by currently enrolled parents. For example, if the ESAs are used primarily by current parents, the funds do help the current parents pay less out of pocket than they otherwise would, but the school doesn't enroll more students or take in more revenue. In other words, many current families using ESAs would still enroll without them. Leveraging ESAs could help in cases of current families who aren't already using an ESA but are at risk of leaving the school for financial reasons. If the ESA can keep them enrolled, the school reduces attrition (and financial) risk. In order to assess whether ESAs can expand or bolster the school's revenue stream, it would be helpful to know how many families would really fall into these categories.

In addition, schools that enroll or recruit families who receive ESA funding must also consider policies on how to treat the funds when determining financial aid eligibility. Would the money count as financial aid from the state and thus offset what the school might otherwise offer? Or would it be treated as a resource to assist parents in affording the family contribution calculated by the school, without adjusting any aid the school has granted?

Last, a school enrolling students with this funding needs to be clear about any government-based requirements (from reporting to testing to program)—requirements that might create onerous administrative burdens and/or compromise the school's mission.

As Chapter 3 also notes, questions like these—as well as many others that government initiatives raise—are not to be taken lightly. The key is to make sure that whatever the school does to sustain its finances also aligns with and sustains its mission.

QUESTIONS TO ASK

- What is your school's unique value proposition? How do you communicate about it with current and prospective families? How well does your value proposition align with their needs? If the answer is "not very well," what changes do you need to make?
- How might you build a staffing and budget model that is able to flex up and down as enrollment and revenue streams move outside of your plans or expectations?
- In what new ways can you take full advantage of opportunities to diversify revenue streams and increase fundraising from key constituents?
- To what degree does your price help or hurt your ability to attract and retain mission-aligned students? What levers can you pull in the financial model to respond to affordability pressures while still generating resources needed for delivering a high-quality program?

STEPS TO TAKE

- Use NAIS's Market View to understand the income and demographic realities of your market. Understand how they relate to the competition the school faces, what parents' choices are, and how they make them.
- Collaborate with your school's enrollment and business managers to set three- to five-year budget plans that reflect movement toward an intentional financial sustainability plan.
- Examine the population projections at play for the market. Create budget scenarios that anticipate the best, worst, and most-likely outcomes in enrollment from year to year. Identify the staffing and program

adjustments that would be necessary to have a balanced budget under each scenario.

- Engage the advancement office in design thinking around engaging underutilized supporters in the school's community, especially alumni.

MORE TO EXPLORE

Access further information here.

"Jobs-to-Be-Done Study on Independent School Donors," NAIS:
https://www.nais.org/articles/pages/research/nais-research-jobs-to-be-done-study-on-independent-schools-donors/

"Jobs-to-Be-Done Study on Independent School Parents," NAIS:
https://www.nais.org/articles/pages/research/nais-research-jobs-to-be-done-study-on-independent-school-parents/

NAIS Data and Analysis for School Leadership (DASL):
https://dasl.nais.org

NAIS Market View:
https://marketview.nais.org

Strategy Lab Financial Series Workshops, NAIS:
https://strategylab.nais.org/

ENDNOTES

[1] Don Soifer, National Microschooling Center, quoted in Rick Hess, "What the Heck Are Microschools?" *Education Week*, May 31, 2023; online at https://www.edweek.org/policy-politics/opinion-what-the-heck-are-microschools/2023/05.

[2] U.S. Census Bureau, "Education Table 1. School Enrollment Type for Children in Kindergarten to Twelfth Grade, by Select Characteristics," Household Pulse Survey, April 30 to May 27, 2024; online at https://www.census.gov/data/tables/2024/demo/hhp/cycle05.html.

[3] NAIS, "Jobs-to-Be-Done Study on Independent School Parents"; online at https://www.nais.org/articles/pages/research/nais-research-jobs-to-be-done-study-on-independent-school-parents/.

[4] National Center for Education Statistics, "Homeschooled Children and Reasons for Homeschooling," *Condition of Education* (Washington, DC: U.S. Department of Education, Institute of Education Sciences, 2022); online at https://nces.ed.gov/programs/coe/indicator/tgk.

[5] NAIS Demographic Center, "Summary Trend Report and Analysis, 2023, U.S. Total."

ON THE HORIZON

Flexibility and contingency planning remain vital. With the uncertainty that accompanies a presidential election year and the possible ensuing transition to a new federal administration, financial markets may be unsteady. This climate could impact the performance of schools' endowment funds and other investment income streams.

Families' mixed feelings about the economy will continue to shape their choices. Consumer confidence levels have yet to return to pre-pandemic rates. This economic uncertainty is likely to influence families' perceptions of independent school affordability amid other major financial decisions they're weighing.

New generations are bringing new hopes and fears. Shifts in preferences, values, and motivations among millennials (born between 1981 and 1996) can flavor everything from their child-bearing plans to what they expect independent schools to deliver—all of which will affect schools' financial stability.

[6] Board of Governors of the Federal Reserve System, “Summary of Economic Projections,” Figure 3E, June 12, 2024; online at https://www.federalreserve.gov/monetarypolicy/files/fomcprojtabl20240612.pdf.

[7] Sylvia Allegretto, “Teacher Pay Penalty Still Looms Large,” Economic Policy Institute, September 29, 2023; online at https://www.epi.org/publication/teacher-pay-in-2022/.

[8] NAIS, Data and Analysis for School Leadership (DASL).

[9] Ibid.

[10] EdChoice, “School Choice Facts and Statistics”; online at https:/www.edchoice.org/school-choice/fast-facts/.

2

The Workforce Forecast

By Brenna Foley and Amada Torres

Brenna Foley is a research analyst at NAIS.

Amada Torres is vice president for studies, insights, and research.

Key Takeaways

- Schools will continue to face challenges with attracting and retaining teachers. However, a source of some new hires may be at hand as public schools cut positions.
- To retain their teachers, school leaders are looking at ways to make teachers' jobs more manageable and rewarding. Possibilities include thoughtful use of artificial intelligence and experiments with team teaching and four-day workweeks.
- New demands mean teachers need new and different professional development. In addition to technology training, this could include better new-teacher orientation and guidance related to students' mental health challenges. Most of all, professional development needs to be relevant to what teachers say they need.

Teacher Shortages Are Here to Stay

Many schools across the country have been facing faculty hiring and retention challenges for the past several years. Cultural, political, and economic changes have led to a decline in the number of available, high-quality teachers. By 2022, there were at least 36,000 vacant teaching positions in U.S. public schools along with 163,000 positions held by underqualified teachers.[1] Similarly, in the fall of 2023, 15.5% of independent schools were reporting unfilled teaching positions at the beginning of the school year.[2]

FIGURE 1

As School Started in 2023, Independent Schools Nationwide Faced Teacher Shortages

NAIS MEMBER SCHOOLS REPORTING UNFILLED TEACHING POSITIONS, SEPTEMBER 2023 BY REGION

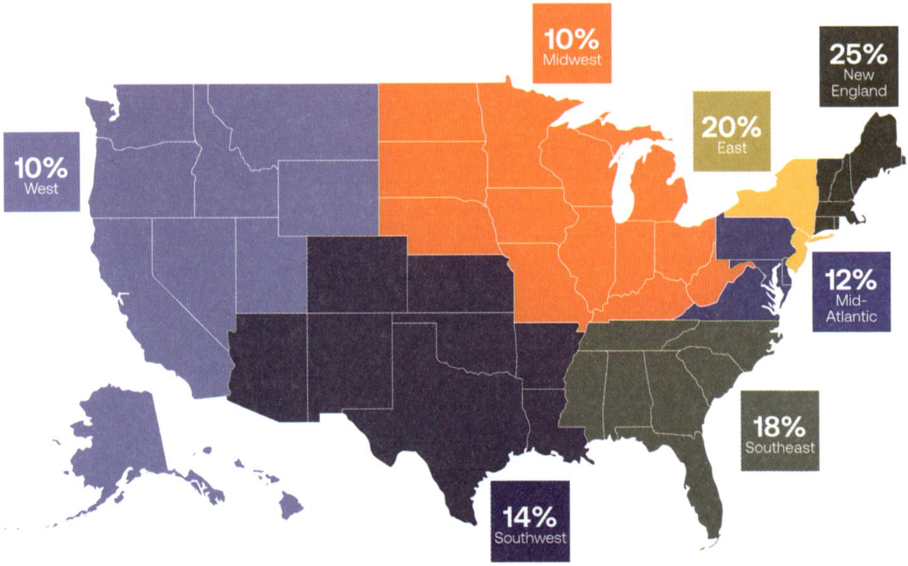

Source: NAIS Snapshot Survey, "Hiring at a Glance," September 2023

One of the leading causes of the teacher shortage is a narrowing pipeline. Fifty years ago, more than 20% of college graduates received their degree in education. Since then the number of college students has grown 150%, but the number of education majors has fallen almost 50%.[3] A survey of high school and college students who had taken the ACT test found several reasons for their lack of interest in pursuing teaching, with 63% citing low pay as the top reason. Other reasons included lack of opportunity for career growth (43%), lack of respect for teachers (30%), and too little flexibility for teaching styles (28%).[4] Additionally, women have traditionally received the majority of education degrees, but as new career opportunities opened up for women, fewer were interested in pursuing a degree in education.[5]

Another factor contributing to the teacher shortage in 2022-2023 and 2023-2024 was a flurry of hiring at public schools. During the pandemic, the government allocated about $190 billion to public schools in emergency aid. Schools used these funds for sanitation and enrichment programs and to create and fill positions. However, funding for these programs runs out in September 2024, right at the beginning of the school year for most, and public schools will need to assess where to cut costs. A quarter of public schools have no revenue to replace the emergency funding, while other schools expect to use state funding and local taxes.[6] For some public school teachers, the loss of this funding could mean losing their positions.[7] A June 2023 survey by AASA, the School Superintendents Association, found that about half of the public schools reported that they would have to cut specialist positions, such as tutors and reading coaches.[8]

It's possible that independent schools could find themselves receiving more applications from qualified candidates who previously worked at public schools. However, to become employers of choice, independent schools will need to revisit their recruiting efforts.

One thing that could help attract top talent is addressing the obstacles that prevent individuals from pursuing teaching careers, such as low salaries and limited opportunities for advancement. Competitive pay may be a priority since teachers' salaries have not kept pace with those of other professions. In 2022, teachers made 26.4% less on average than professionals with similar education.[9] Emphasizing the flexibility and creativity of teaching in independent schools may also help attract candidates.

Revisiting the Teacher's Role Is Key to Addressing Teacher Morale and Burnout

Evaluating the teacher's role holistically could help schools attract and retain great teachers. A recent Pew Research study of public school teachers found that only a third of the respondents were extremely or very satisfied with their jobs, compared to more than half of all employed adults. When asked about several aspects of their job, fewer than half of the respondents said that they felt extremely or very satisfied with their freedom to implement the curriculum, their relationship with students' parents, and their benefits and salaries.[10]

Teachers responding to the Pew survey also indicated that they do not have enough time in the workday to accomplish all that is expected of them.[11] These expectations can be daunting. An *Education Week* national survey found that while teachers work an average of 57 hours a week, only 33 of these hours are spent teaching, preparing lessons, and grading.[12] It is not surprising that almost eight out of 10 teachers in the Pew study said that their job is frequently stressful, and about seven in 10 described it as overwhelming.[13]

NAIS has found that independent school teachers express similar sentiments. More than 50% find their job often or always stressful, and over 90% report more than 40 hours of work during a typical week, with 25% working more than 60 hours (Figure 2).[14]

How can school leaders make the teacher's job more manageable and rewarding? In responding to *EdWeek*'s survey, teachers discussed tasks they wish could be removed from their plates:

- Finding or acting as substitutes
- Collecting and analyzing student data
- Helping new teachers
- Keeping parents in the loop on everything

FIGURE 2

Working More Than 40 Hours Weekly Is a Given for the Vast Majority of Independent School Teachers

HOURS PER WEEK THAT TEACHERS WORK, NOVEMBER 2023

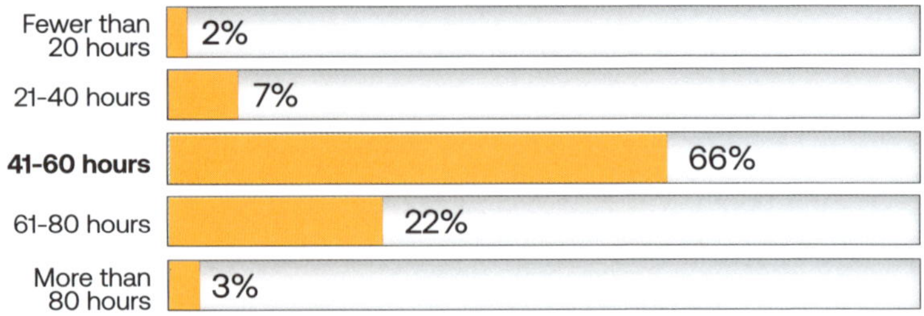

Source: NAIS Snapshot Survey, "Teacher Retention at a Glance," November 2023

- Participating in school community events
- Taking on janitorial duties
- Taking on noninstructional duties[15]

Artificial intelligence (AI) could help alleviate some of the pressures on teachers. This new technology has shown some downsides, such as producing inaccurate or biased responses, and it raises concerns about data privacy. But educators are experimenting with ways that AI tools can help them become more efficient. For instance, some teachers use ChatGPT and other generative AI tools to develop lesson plans, rubrics, assignments, or materials for students. Others use AI to compose emails to parents or write letters of recommendation for students. In a January 2024 NAIS Snapshot Survey, 45% of teachers said they had not used AI for administrative tasks. But respondents who had employed AI said they used it for planning lessons, writing student comments, doing research, and composing emails (Figure 3).[16] Read more on this topic in Chapter 6, "The Artificial Intelligence Forecast."

Some school leaders are experimenting with structural changes intended to ease the burden on teachers.

FIGURE 3

NAIS Teachers Are Gradually Adopting AI for Lesson Planning and Other Tasks

TEACHERS RESPOND TO HOW OFTEN THEY HAVE USED AI FOR THE FOLLOWING ADMINISTRATIVE TASKS AS OF JANUARY 2024

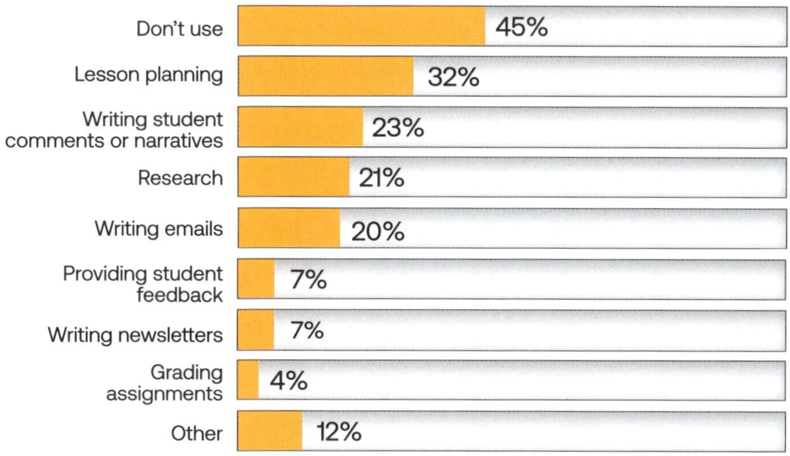

Source: NAIS Snapshot Survey, "AI in Classrooms at a Glance," January 2024

For instance, a number of school districts have implemented team teaching, a model in which two or more teachers share responsibility for the same group of students. In recent years, Arizona State University (ASU) has partnered with public school districts that are interested in moving away from the "one teacher, one classroom" model. ASU is currently working on this with 28 school districts in a dozen states, especially in the western United States. Early research indicates that team teaching improves teacher retention as well as students' performance on reading and mathematics.[17]

Another structural change that has grown more popular since the pandemic is the four-day week approach. This trend is driven by younger generations, particularly Gen Z and millennials. Increasingly, workers want to be assessed and evaluated not by the number of hours they work per week or the time they spend in the workplace but rather by the outcomes they produce.[18]

In K-12 education, the four-day week might boost teacher recruitment and retention by providing the flexibility many teachers desire. As of September 2023, 900 school districts nationwide had adopted a four-day week model, up from 650 districts in 2019.[19]

But while educators and even parents support this approach, four-day weeks have yielded mixed academic outcomes. Some studies have found lower reading and math achievement in districts with four-day weeks. However, researchers also reported that districts that maintained a high level of instruction time did not see the reduced achievement.[20] To avoid reducing instructional time, some schools with four-day weeks have extended the school day from 8 a.m. to 3:45 p.m.[21] In other cases, schools are open five days a week, but faculty schedules are modified to accommodate a four-day week for them. In still other schools, teacher workweeks have been modified so that teachers are working five days but in the classroom four days. The fifth day is used for planning, teacher meetings, grading, and other obligations.[22]

New Technologies and Job Demands Will Require Revamping Professional Development and Training

Technological developments are moving faster than ever. Artificial intelligence, virtual reality, and machine learning have made significant strides in just the past few years. Children are using these technologies daily and are much quicker to adopt and become proficient with them than adults.

However, many schools are struggling to make use of new technologies. As mentioned above, almost half of the independent school teachers responding to an NAIS Snapshot Survey have not used AI to assist with any administrative tasks, and 69% have not incorporated AI into their curriculum. This relatively low use of AI may stem from insufficient training on how to use these tools effectively and appropriately. About 50% of teachers have not received any professional development on artificial intelligence from their school, and 56% have not sought out such professional development. Furthermore, many independent schools do not have any policies regarding AI.[23]

But the professional development challenges schools need to address extend beyond the use of new technologies. The transition into the profession for new teachers or those switching careers is much more complex now. For one thing, classrooms today are different spaces, with cellphones and social media as increasingly troublesome distractions. Students have changed as well. The pandemic exacerbated disruptive behavior and absenteeism, which contributed to learning loss. Offering new teachers a mentor or the support of a team could help.[24] Veteran teachers could assist with classroom management, while other teachers could provide feedback on subject-specific plans.

Teachers must believe that PD is genuinely essential to career growth, not a waste of time.

Student mental health issues have also grown since the pandemic. Teachers may require more training on trauma-responsive practices and methods to create a safe classroom environment.[25] Teaching emotional literacy and focusing on building resilience can also help reduce student mental health problems.[26] However, school leaders should be careful not to make teachers' already busy days even busier, and they should explore ways to leverage school resources to support teachers in these areas.

Finally, when it comes to professional development and training, giving teachers a stronger voice in planning these activities is crucial; almost half of the teachers in the *Education Week* survey said that the professional development they receive is irrelevant.[27] Professional development can help teachers stay current with best practices and improve their teaching skills. But teachers must believe that the training is genuinely essential to their career growth and their effectiveness in the classroom or they will feel that their time has been wasted.

QUESTIONS TO ASK

- How do you identify the reasons teachers are attracted to your school? What are the main reasons teachers leave? What strategies do you have in place to attract and retain faculty?
- How satisfied are the faculty and staff at your school? What are the drivers behind this level of satisfaction? What measurements can you implement to improve satisfaction levels?
- How do your staff perceive your current salaries and benefits compared to those of other public and private schools in your area? What nonmonetary incentives could you offer? How can you make sure your compensation packages remain competitive?
- What opportunities exist for your school to provide a more flexible and supportive working environment? How could you implement some of these opportunities?
- What are your current policies regarding AI used at school and in classrooms? What type of professional development or training could you provide to help teachers familiarize themselves with this new technology?
- How do you identify professional development needs? How do you ensure that faculty receive the type of training they consider essential?
- How might the new demands of the job require independent school leaders to rethink the skills and characteristics they prioritize in the hiring process?

STEPS TO TAKE

- Evaluate teacher compensation and benefits. Make sure they remain as competitive as possible within your market.
- Consider using a survey instrument to measure faculty engagement so that teachers can share what is working and not working at your school.
- Consider using employee feedback to drive your school's decisions about what benefits to offer. New

benefits such as onsite massage services and wellness classes could be added. Some large schools are even offering onsite dental and mobile mammography clinics as a way for teachers to save time while providing them with important wellness and health services.[28]

- Identify all the typical tasks that teachers at your school are required to do and assess which ones could be reassigned or eliminated. Discuss with faculty and staff the ways they could use generative AI tools in the classroom to lessen teachers' workload.
- Based on your school's mission and culture, evaluate whether and how your school could implement team teaching or four-day workweeks for teachers.
- Assess whether the professional development your school offers aligns with what teachers want and need and what your school needs. Regularly identify teachers who could be tapped for leadership opportunities.

MORE TO EXPLORE

Access further information here.

NAIS Career Center:
https://careers.nais.org

NAIS Data and Analysis for School Leadership (DASL):
https://dasl.nais.org

"Overworked and Undervalued: Retaining Top Educators," Liz Kuncl and Kyle Christensen, GALLUP:
https://www.gallup.com/education/609422/overworked-undervalued-retaining-top-educators.aspx

"The State of Teaching," *Education Week*:
https://www.edweek.org/the-state-of-teaching

"Using Artificial Intelligence Tools in K-12 Classrooms," Melissa Kay Diliberti et al., RAND:
https://www.rand.org/content/dam/rand/pubs/research_reports/RRA900/RRA956-21/RAND_RRA956-21.pdf

"What's It Like to Be a Teacher in America Today?" Luona Lin, Kim Parker, and Juliana Menasce Horowitz, Pew Research Center:
https://www.pewresearch.org/social-trends/2024/04/04/whats-it-like-to-be-a-teacher-in-america-today/

ON THE HORIZON

The "gray tsunami" is coming. By 2030, all baby boomers—born from 1946 through 1964—will be 65 years old or older, reaching traditional retirement age.[29] During the period from 2024 to 2030, an estimated 30.4 million Americans will reach the age of 65.[30] All organizations, including independent schools, need to plan to avoid staff disruptions as many individuals enter their senior years.

Younger workers will have new workplace expectations. Gen Zers—born between 1997 and 2012—are expected to overtake baby boomers in the full-time workforce this year,[31] and the generation's representation is expected to grow to 51 million by 2030.[32] This new generation values a diverse and inclusive workplace culture; prioritizes mental health; communicates openly and honestly; wants professional growth; and values collaboration, autonomy, and flexibility.[33] Independent schools will need to offer an environment that attracts and retains these new employees.

Interest in unions appears to be growing. While unions are not typical in independent schools, interest seems to have increased in recent years. Teachers may believe that forming a union can boost their power to negotiate for better salaries and improved working conditions.

ENDNOTES

[1] Tuan D. Nguyen, Chanh B. Lam, and Paul Bruno, "Is There a National Teacher Shortage? A Systematic Examination of Reports of Teacher Shortages in the United States," EdWorkingPaper No. 22-631, Annenberg/Brown University, August 2022; online at https://edworkingpapers.com/sites/default/files/ai22-631.pdf.

[2] NAIS Snapshot Survey, "Hiring at a Glance," September 2023; online at https://www.nais.org/getmedia/025b296f-14f6-43f8-b3ef-6da67cc1e16a/NAIS-Research_Snapshot-Survey-Hiring_9-26-23.pdf.

[3] Aimee Picchi and Sanvi Bangalore, "Education Was Once the No. 1 Major for College Students. Now It's an Afterthought," CBS MoneyWatch, July 2023; online at https://tinyurl.com/mr99w6am.

[4] Michelle Croft, Gretchen Guffy, and Dan Vitale, "Encouraging More High School Students to Consider Teaching," ACT Research and Policy, Issue Brief, June 2018; online at https://www.act.org/content/dam/act/unsecured/documents/pdfs/Encouraging-More-HS-Students-to-Consider-Teaching.pdf.

[5] Nguyen et al., "Is There a National Teacher Shortage?"

[6] Lexi Lonas, "Schools Stare Down Deadline as COVID-19 Relief Funds Set to Expire," *The Hill*, March 12, 2024; online at https://thehill.com/homenews/education/4524244-schools-deadline-covid-19-relief-funds-esser/.

[7] Edunomics Lab, "A Timely Update from the Edunomics Lab at Georgetown's McCourt School," n.d.; online at https://us19.campaign-archive.com/?u=179e2a9db6ce62a03ab6a0a74&id=94269f9630.

[8] Hannah Dellinger, Matt Barnum, and Collin Binkley, "Schools Are Cutting Recovery Programs as U.S. Aid Money Dries Up. Students Are Still Struggling," *Chalkbeat*, September 2023; online at https://www.chalkbeat.org/2023/9/6/23851143/covid-relief-schools-esser-spending-learning-loss/.

[9] National Education Association, "Educator Pay Data 2024: Starting Teacher Salaries," April 2024; online at https://www.nea.org/resource-library/educator-pay-and-student-spending-how-does-your-state-rank/starting-teacher.

[10] Luona Lin, Kim Parker, and Juliana Menasce Horowitz, "What's It Like to Be a Teacher in America Today?" Pew Research Center, April 4, 2024; online at https://www.pewresearch.org/social-trends/2024/04/04/whats-it-like-to-be-a-teacher-in-america-today/.

[11] Ibid.

[12] Madeline Will, "Dear Administrators: Teachers Want You to Get These 8 Tasks Off Their Plates," *Education Week*, March 29, 2024; online at https://www.edweek.org/teaching-learning/dear-administrators-teachers-want-you-to-get-these-8-tasks-off-their-plates/2024/03?utm_source.

[13] Lin et al., "What's It Like to Be a Teacher in America Today?"

[14] NAIS Snapshot Survey, "Teacher Retention at a Glance," November-December 2023; online at https://www.nais.org/getmedia/1bfba474-5d98-4708-b6fa-3d662e39d33f/NAIS-Research_Snapshot-Survey-Teacher-Wellbeing_12-8-23.pdf.

[15] Will, "Dear Administrators."

[16] NAIS Snapshot Survey, "AI in Classrooms at a Glance," January-February 2024; online at https://www.nais.org/getmedia/6baf64a8-ecfd-4e9c-ac3c-69a9f3971491/NAISsnapshotSurveyAIinClassrooms021224.pdf.

[17] Neal Morton, "Are Two Teachers Better Than One? More Schools Say Yes to Team Teaching," *The Hechinger Report*, April 25, 2024; online at https://hechingerreport.org/are-two-teachers-better-than-one-more-schools-say-yes-to-team-teaching/.

[18] Ece Yildirim, "Over 75% of U.S. Workers Say They Could Complete the Same Amount of Work in 4 Days Rather Than 5," CNBC Make It, November 3, 2023; online at https://www.cnbc.com/2023/11/03/over-75percent-of-us-workers-say-they-productive-4-days-rather-than-5.html.

[19] Caitlynn Peetz, "The Popularity of 4-Day School Weeks, in Charts," *Education Week*, January 23, 2024; online at https://www.edweek.org/leadership/the-popularity-of-4-day-school-weeks-in-charts/2024/01.

[20] Sarah D. Sparks, "4 Studies to Know on 4-Day School Weeks," *Education Week*, February 14, 2023; online at https://www.edweek.org/leadership/four-studies-to-know-on-four-day-school-weeks/2023/02.

[21] Alexandria Fisher, "Indiana School Becomes First in State to Move to 4-Day School Week," NBC Chicago, April 22, 2024; online at https://www.nbcchicago.com/news/local/indiana-school-becomes-first-in-state-to-move-to-4-day-school-week/3417278/.

[22] Jackie Valley, "Could Four-Day Weeks Lead to More Progress for Students?" *The Christian Science Monitor*, September 20, 2023; online at https://www.csmonitor.com/USA/Education/2023/0920/Could-four-day-weeks-lead-to-more-progress-for-students.

[23] NAIS Snapshot Survey, "AI in Classrooms at a Glance."

[24] Olina Banerji, "'I Probably Cried Every Night': The Truth About Supporting New Teachers," *Education Week*, March 6, 2024; online at https://www.edweek.org/teaching-learning/i-probably-cried-every-night-the-truth-about-supporting-new-teachers/2024/03.

[25] Rachael Kingrey, "Addressing Student Mental Health: Strategies for Teachers," *The Chronicle of Evidence-Based Mentoring* (reprinted from the American Youth Policy Institute, November 9, 2022); online at https://www.evidencebasedmentoring.org/addressing-student-mental-health-strategies-for-teachers/.

[26] Holly Korbey, "What's the Role of Teachers in Supporting Student Mental Health?" Edutopia, October 21, 2022; online at https://www.edutopia.org/article/the-doctor-is-in-your-classroom.

[27] Lesli A. Maxwell and Vanessa Solis, "Principals, Are You in Sync with Your Teachers?" *Education Week*, March 6, 2024; online at https://www.edweek.org/leadership/principals-are-you-in-sync-with-your-teachers-downloadable/2024/03.

[28] Elizabeth Heubeck, "Massages, Mammograms, and Dental Care: How One School Saves Teachers' Time," *Education Week*, May 10, 2024; online at https://www.edweek.org/teaching-learning/massages-mammograms-and-dental-care-how-one-school-saves-teachers-time/2024/05.

[29] America Counts Staff, "By 2030, All Baby Boomers Will Be Age 65 or Older: 2020 Census Will Help Policymakers Prepare for the Incoming Wave of Aging Boomers," U.S. Census Bureau, December 10, 2019; online at https://www.census.gov/library/stories/2019/12/by-2030-all-baby-boomers-will-be-age-65-or-older.html.

[30] Maurie Backman, "Are You Turning 65 Between 2024 and 2030 and Not Financially Prepared for Retirement? Do This," *USA Today*, May 7, 2024; online at https://www.usatoday.com/story/money/2024/05/07/most-americans-turning-65-between-2024-and-2030-arent-financially-prepared-for-retirement-do-this-if/73568014007/.

[31] Aaron Terrazas and Daniel Zhao, "Glassdoor's 2024 Workplace Trends," Glassdoor, November 15, 2023; online at https://www.glassdoor.com/research/workplace-trends-2024.

[32] Naomi Nix, "Gen Z Workers to Triple by 2030, Snap-Commissioned Report Says," Bloomberg, March 10, 2021; online at https://www.bloomberg.com/news/articles/2021-03-10/gen-z-workers-to-triple-by-2030-snap-commissioned-report-says.

[33] Angel Odukoya, "The Changing Generational Values," Johns Hopkins University, November 17, 2022; online at https://imagine.jhu.edu/blog/2022/11/17/the-changing-generational-values/.

3

The Legal and Legislative Forecast

By Myra McGovern and Whitney Silverman

Myra McGovern is vice president of external relations at NAIS.

Whitney Silverman is assistant legal counsel and director of government relations.

Key Takeaways

- Private school choice programs, which hold both promise and challenges for independent schools, are likely to keep expanding. Most growth will occur at the state level.
- Tax legislation could affect nonprofits in the year ahead. But the traditional understanding of independent schools' nonprofit status appears safe for now.
- Topics ranging from parental rights to school safety will continue to be on the agenda for state and federal lawmakers.

State School Choice Bills Continue to Grow

Independent school leaders have a clear incentive to keep a close eye on private school choice legislation—legislation that provides financial support to families to help pay for their children's education outside their local public schools. Choice programs may give independent schools an opportunity to increase enrollment,[1] supplement their existing financial aid efforts, and expand diversity initiatives. However, historically some in independent schools have expressed concern that these programs may restrict the independence of their schools, not align with their mission or philosophy, or not provide enough financial sustainability to support new students.

Enrollment increases that school choice could bring about may differ for different schools and will depend on the scope of each state's programs. Schools should guard against trying to grow too quickly—or rushing toward new programs as a method of stabilizing finances—if a choice initiative's long-term future is uncertain.[2] Most important, schools should evaluate each program opportunity carefully to determine whether it aligns with the school's mission and supports continued independence.

Here is an overview of what's happening in private school choice programs as of the *Trendbook*'s press date in summer 2024.

School choice programs are growing and are likely to continue to grow in the 2024-2025 school year and beyond. As of July 2024, 34 states and the District of Columbia offered at least one type of private school choice initiative (Figure 1).[3] There are at least 75 different programs that serve an estimated 1,038,487 students across the United States.[4]

Each state's initiatives have unique criteria for eligibility. For example, many are targeted toward students with disabilities, families below certain income levels, or students who previously attended public schools. Some are "universal school choice" programs—that is, they have few conditions and are available to most students in the state. In addition, each state's programs vary in whether they place conditions on participating students and schools, such as testing mandates, state approval, staffing requirements, or other reporting obligations.

Overall, choice programs fall into three main categories:

- **Vouchers:** States provide a set amount of money that can be used for private school tuition. Vouchers may be offered to parents or

FIGURE 1

The Majority of States Have Private School Choice Programs

STATES WITH AT LEAST ONE INITIATIVE

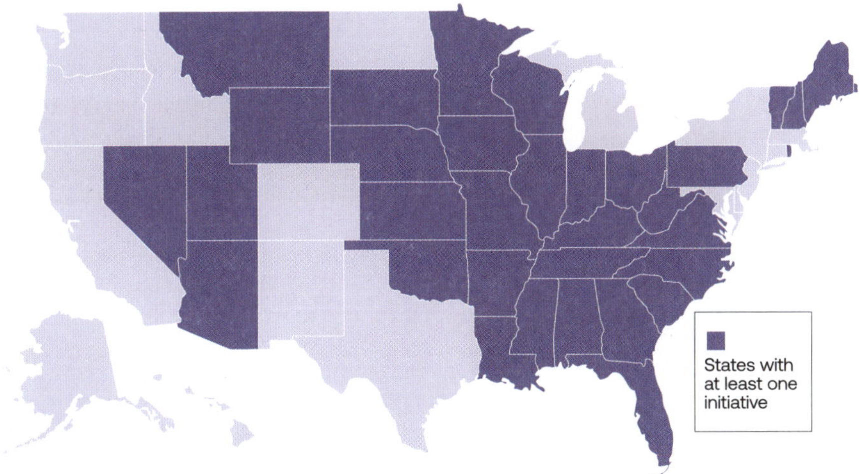

Sources: Hoover Institution, "Map of School Choice Options Available by State"; Libby Stanford et al., "Which States Have Private School Choice," *Education Week*; EdChoice, "School Choice in America Dashboard"

paid directly to the school.*

- **Education savings accounts (ESAs):** State governments make deposits into savings accounts that families can use to pay for approved expenses, such as private school tuition, tutoring, online programs, instructional materials, homeschooling supplies, and more.
- **Tax credit scholarships:** Individuals or businesses receive a tax benefit for donating to a designated scholarship-granting organization (SGO). The SGO then provides scholarships to students for private school tuition.[5]

A May 2024 NAIS survey offers a view of how NAIS member schools regard private school choice programs.[6]

Among respondents whose schools are located in states or municipalities that offer programs, 44.3% participated in a school choice program in 2023-2024 (Figure 2). Tax credit scholarship programs were most popular,

* *Town tuitioning programs*, a subset of voucher programs, are found mostly in northern New England. In these programs, towns that do not have their own public school pay a certain amount of tuition to the private schools that students attend.

FIGURE 2

Fewer Than Half of NAIS Member Schools in Areas with School Choice Initiatives Participate in Them

EDUCATOR RESPONSES TO THE SURVEY QUESTIONS...

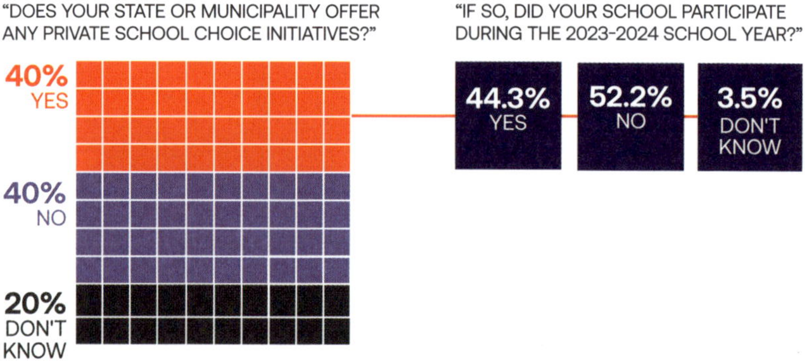

Source: Phillip Brooks, "NAIS Government Programs Survey," NAIS

with 50% of schools participating. Next were voucher programs at 34%, followed by education savings account programs at 18%. Among the reasons respondents gave for participating were to support more students (particularly low-income families) and to increase the diversity of their student body.[7]

The 52.2% of schools that did not participate in an available school choice program cited concerns about compliance requirements and a desire to maintain independence from government, among other reasons.[8]

Although almost all school choice action has been in the states, there is some activity on the federal level. One federal school choice program called the Opportunity Scholarship Program is available for students who live in Washington, DC.[9] It's possible that Congress will expand the DC Opportunity Scholarship Program, which is funded under the SOAR Act (Scholarships for Opportunity and Results). The 118th Congress (2023-2024) introduced legislation to permanently authorize and expand the program. But this legislation did not gain traction and is unlikely to become law in the near term, particularly if Democrats retain control of at least one chamber and/or the White House.[10]

Over the last few years, the federal school choice focus has been on a federal tax credit for donors who make contributions to a scholarship-granting organization, which would then provide scholarships to students. At this time, the Educational Choice for Children Act has 151 cosponsors in the House and 31 cosponsors in the Senate.[11] This program would expand school choice options to families who do not have programs in their states. The legislation, however, has not received a floor vote in either chamber. While a Republican president in 2025 would work to expand school choice if elected,[12] there was no significant federal movement on school choice during 2017-2021 beyond the expansion of 529 programs through tax reform in 2017 to include expenses for K-12 education.[†]

But again, it is very likely that school choice efforts will continue to expand—and especially education savings accounts. After the first ESA was created in 2011, the estimated number of students using ESAs rose steadily with the biggest increase happening from 2022 (40,205 students) to 2024 (328,741 students).[13] The flexibility of ESAs is attractive to many families, who can use them for tuition and other types of education expenses. Additionally, many ESA programs have broader eligibility criteria than many voucher programs, allowing ESAs to serve more families.

Whether and how to embrace school choice programs is a decision each independent school has to weigh for itself. As with any decision, a school's focus should be on its educational program and adherence to mission.

Tax Legislation Could Affect Nonprofits in the Year Ahead, While the Traditional Understanding of Independent Schools' Nonprofit Status Looks Safe for Now

Choice initiatives aren't the only form of legislation likely to impact independent schools in the year ahead.

Tax law changes could further affect the deductibility of charitable gifts. Federal tax policy is set for a big year in 2024 and 2025. Congress will have to decide whether to extend the changes ushered in with the 2017 Tax Cuts and Jobs Act (TCJA), let the changes expire, or make other changes by the end of 2025.[14]

Among other changes, the TCJA increased the standard deduction

[†] A 529 plan is a savings account created by a family or individual for a child's education expenses. Although the account does not receive direct federal funding, the earnings are not taxed as long as the account is used for qualifying education expenses. In addition, many states exempt contributions to these plans from an individual's income for the purpose of state taxes.

and enacted a $10,000 limit on the amount of state and local taxes that can be deducted.[15] Since those who do not itemize do not receive federal tax benefits for donating to charity, nonprofits—including independent schools—were concerned that these changes would reduce charitable giving due to decreased incentives. Although a number of factors (including the COVID-19 pandemic) may have played a part, giving to charities of most types has in fact been declining since 2021, and the overall number of donors is decreasing.[16] To help combat these trends and provide incentives for broader charitable giving across income levels, there is an ongoing bipartisan effort to enact a universal charitable deduction.[17]

As Congress debates what to do about the tax provisions set to expire in 2025, other topics of concern to independent schools may be back in the news in the months ahead. These could include tuition remission, protection of employer-provided tuition assistance, support for tax-exempt bonds, and employer-provided housing—all benefits that were on the chopping block during the legislative debates around the TCJA.

Judicial threats to independent schools' tax-exempt status may continue, although recent court rulings have been positive. Several cases emerged between 2022 and 2024 that questioned whether nonprofit status in and of itself constituted federal financial assistance.[18] These cases posed a threat for several reasons. Among the most prominent: Most independent schools rely on their nonprofit status and charitable contributions. Further, many schools decline to accept federal financial assistance because doing so triggers a host of complex and ever-changing regulatory burdens.

Thankfully, judges in two recent cases—including one at the circuit court level—ruled that tax exemption is not a form of federal financial assistance.[19] In addition, the Safeguarding Charities Act has been introduced on Capitol Hill to explicitly state the same thing.[20] However, as of press time, that bill does not have bipartisan support and is unlikely to become law soon. So more cases of this variety may emerge in district and circuit courts around the country in the coming years.

K-12 Education Will Continue to Be a Flashpoint of Legislative Activity

Other issues affecting the K-12 education space are also likely to see legislative activity.

One area of great interest involves the intersection of race, LGBTQ+ rights, curriculum, and parental involvement. Over the last few years, hundreds of bills have been introduced that would restrict or limit discussions of race and DEI in schools, use of preferred pronouns and names, and discussions and teaching about sexuality and gender identity. Some of these bills also wove in the concept of a parental bill of rights. Each state's approach differs slightly, and not all have become law.

Many of these bills require parental notification regarding issues of sexuality and gender identity and the ability to review (and perhaps object to) curriculum and policies.[21] Most bills apply only to public schools—but not all. For example, a bill the Georgia legislature considered (but did not act on) applied to both public and private schools. However, there is at least one bill this year—in Idaho—that was enacted into law and prohibits certain types of books in public and private schools alike.[22] Independent schools should be on the lookout for related activity in their state legislatures in the year ahead, particularly if more states look to include private schools in these mandates.

The outcomes of state and local elections will have the greatest influence on these types of bills over the next several years. But the 2024 presidential election is also likely to shape future policy related to gender and parental rights. If Democrats retain the presidency, the administration will continue efforts to enforce Title IX as it pertains to gender identity and sexual orientation.[23] If the White House shifts to Republicans, that administration will roll back Biden-era efforts and will likely renew attempts to pass a federal parental bill of rights, at least as it pertains to public schools.[24]

Legislation further addressing school safety and mental health is also possible—and may be an area of potential bipartisan agreement. The Bipartisan Safer Communities Act was signed into law in June 2022 after mass shootings at Robb Elementary School in Uvalde, Texas, and Tops Supermarket in Buffalo, New York. Legislators were able to work together to fund a range of initiatives that included support for school safety and mental health programs, which offered opportunities for private schools as well.[25]

The bill stayed away from many of the most contentious issues, and there is still significant division around issues such as arming teachers—which some states are doing.[26] But the legislation has been hailed as a breakthrough on a topic that has long been mired in partisan division and

ON THE HORIZON

Watch for action related to leave and pay. Efforts to increase access to paid leave and to improve pay equity will continue to increase on the state level.[27] Pay transparency laws will also continue to gain steam.[28]

Privacy and student data privacy are likely to be on lawmakers' agendas. Efforts to enhance comprehensive privacy protections and protections for student data will continue. New regulations for the Children's Online Privacy Protection Act (COPPA) may go into effect in late 2024 or early 2025. Federal efforts for comprehensive privacy reform will continue in Congress.[29]

International student numbers will continue to be in flux post-pandemic. However, while the largest sending country will continue to be China, its dominance will continue to fall while other countries will be on the rise. Control of Congress and the presidency will affect the tone and policy direction of immigration generally and regulations around international students and educators specifically.

may offer a model for federal and state activity in the future.

The 2024-2025 school year promises to be busy on the legislative and regulatory fronts across all 50 states and the federal government. Whether the subject is school choice, tax reform, parental rights, or school safety, there will be many areas for independent school educators to watch. NAIS will continue to track issues and keep members up to date.

QUESTIONS TO ASK

- If your school is weighing participation in a school choice program, think through these questions:
  - How does the program align with your school's mission and values, including areas such as diversity, access, affordability, and independence?
  - What level of financial support does the program provide prospective students? What financial aid does your school have available to supplement the outside assistance?
  - Is the program/funding source sustainable? If the source of funds was not reauthorized, would the students still be able to attend?
  - Does the program place additional requirements on participating private schools beyond current federal and state law?
- How might changes in tax law impact your fundraising goals and methods?
- How do you communicate with school families about what you teach and why? How do you foster strong relationships with students' families?
- What needs does your school have related to safety and well-being? What opportunities are available at the federal and state levels to support or improve your community's safety?

STEPS TO TAKE

- Consider having a discussion at the board level about what type of funding opportunities your school would—and would not—consider.

- Determine whether federal or state laws regarding LGBTQ+ rights or parents' rights apply to independent schools in your state. Regardless, remember the law is a floor, not a ceiling—it sets a minimum standard for what your school should do, not a limit on what your community should expect. Evaluate your enrollment contract, handbook, and other policies to ensure that they are in line with your mission, vision, and values as well as the law.
- Evaluate opportunities to receive security/wellness training, support, technical assistance, resources, or funding. What are the benefits and drawbacks of participation?

MORE TO EXPLORE

Access further information here.

"Legislative Tracker: 2023 Parent-Rights Bills in the States," FutureEd:
https://www.future-ed.org/legislative-tracker-2023-parent-rights-bills-in-the-states/

"Review Your School's Approach to Safety and Security Risk Management," Myra McGovern and Megan Mann, NAIS:
https://www.nais.org/learn/washington-watch/march-2023/review-your-schools-safety-and-security-risk-management-process/

"School Choice in America Dashboard," EdChoice:
https://www.edchoice.org/school-choice-in-america-dashboard-scia/

ENDNOTES

[1] Florida has seen an increase in private school enrollment as school choice efforts have expanded. "Florida's Private Schools: 2022-23 School Year Annual Report," Florida Department of Education; online at https://www.fldoe.org/core/fileparse.php/7562/urlt/PS-AnnualReport2023.pdf.

[2] Michael Q. McShane and Nicole Stelle Garnett, "Implementing K-12 Education Savings Accounts," Manhattan Institute/American Enterprise Institute, June 22, 2023; online at https://www.aei.org/research-products/report/implementing-k-12-education-savings-accounts/. This report, which focuses on ESAs, urges schools to "resist the temptation to simply use ESA funds to shore up shaky finances by filling empty seats. To participate successfully, schools must recruit new students—which necessitates telling parents a compelling story about why [these schools] are the best option for their children." Neal McCluskey, "New Survey: Private School Enrollment Grew from the Last to the Current School Year, But the COVID Boost Might

Be Ending," *Cato at Liberty* blog, Cato Institute, March 26, 2024; online at https://www.cato.org/blog/new-survey-private-school-enrollment-grew-last-current-school-year-covid-boost-might-be-ending.

[3] Hoover Institution, "Map of School Choice Options Available by State" (interactive map); online at https://www.hoover.org/schoolchoicemap. Libby Stanford, Mark Lieberman, and Victoria A. Ifatusin, "Which States Have Private School Choice," *Education Week*, January 31, 2024, updated May 8, 2024; online at https://www.edweek.org/policy-politics/which-states-have-private-school-choice/2024/01. EdChoice, "School Choice in America Dashboard"; online at https://www.edchoice.org/school-choice-in-america-dashboard-scia/.

[4] EdChoice, "How America's Students Access K-12 Education"; online at https://tinyurl.com/5ek3mnsp.

[5] EdChoice, *The ABCs of School Choice, 2024 Edition* (Indianapolis, IN: 2024); online at https://www.edchoice.org/wp-content/uploads/2023/11/2024-ABCs-of-School-Choice.pdf.

[6] Phillip Brooks, "NAIS Government Programs Survey," NAIS, forthcoming.

[7] Ibid.

[8] Ibid.

[9] Serving Our Children, "A Private School Education for Your Child" (DC's Opportunity Scholarship Program); online at https://servingourchildrendc.org/about-us/.

[10] H.R. 3663, 118th Congress (2023-2024), "SOAR Permanent Authorization Act"; online at https://www.congress.gov/bill/118th-congress/house-bill/3663. The Senate version—S. 69—had bipartisan support from the late Senator Dianne Feinstein. At this time, it is unclear whether another Democratic Senator will become a champion of the SOAR Permanent Authorization Act in her place.

[11] H.R. 531, 118th Congress (2023-2024), "Educational Choice for Children Act"; online at https://tinyurl.com/y33t9h3m.

[12] James Oliphant, "Trump, Republicans Push Private School Options to Win Over Parents Across Party Lines," Reuters, December 8, 2023; online at https://www.reuters.com/world/us/trump-republicans-push-private-school-options-win-over-parents-across-party-2023-12-08/.

[13] EdChoice, "School Choice Facts and Statistics"; online at https://www.edchoice.org/school-choice/fast-facts/.

[14] Joint Committee on Taxation, U.S. Congress, "General Explanation of Public Law 115-97," December 2018; online at https://www.jct.gov/getattachment/7c87c9f5-1cb8-4202-a1ca-b608a04c741b/s-1-18-5152.pdf.

[15] Whitney Silverman, "Tax Cuts and Jobs Act—the Final Bill," NAIS Legal Advisory, February 2020; online at https://tinyurl.com/444drakj. Whitney Silverman and Debra Wilson, "SALT Regulations and Potential Impact: A Summary," NAIS Legal Advisory, July 2019; online at https://tinyurl.com/3ysvkrjm.

[16] The Fundraising Effectiveness Project (FEP), "Quarterly Fundraising Report: Year-to-Date Nonprofit Sector Trends," January 1, 2023, to December 31, 2023; online at https://data.givingtuesday.org/fep-report/.

[17] Paul Clolery, "New Congressional Support for a Universal Charitable Deduction," *The NonProfit Times*, May 18, 2023; online at https://thenonprofittimes.com/regulation/new-congressional-support-for-a-universal-charitable-deduction/. S. 566, 118th Congress (2023-2024), "Charitable Act"; online at https://www.congress.gov/bill/118th-congress/senate-bill/566. H.R. 3435, 118th Congress (2023-2024), "Charitable Act"; online at https://www.congress.gov/bill/118th-congress/house-bill/3435. During the COVID-19 pandemic, Congress created a smaller temporary universal charitable deduction that generated $10.9 billion in donations, with 25% coming from those making under $30,000 per year. Office of U.S. Congressman Blake Moore, "Representatives Moore, Davis, Steel, and Pappas Introduce

Legislation to Encourage Charitable Giving and Support Local Communities," Press Release, May 17, 2023; online at https://blakemoore.house.gov/media/press-releases/representatives-moore-davis-steel-and-pappas-introduce-legislation-encourage.

[18] *E.H. v. Valley Christian Academy* (C.D. Cal. July 24, 2022); *Buettner-Hartsoe v. Balt. Lutheran High School Association* (4th Cir. Mar. 27, 2024); and *Doe v. Horne* (D. Ariz. Dec. 11, 2023).

[19] *Buettner-Hartsoe v. Balt. Lutheran High School Association* and *Doe v. Horne*.

[20] H.R. 2707, 118th Congress (2023-2024). "Safeguarding Charities Act"; online at https://www.congress.gov/bill/118th-congress/house-bill/7027. S. 3604, 118th Congress (2023-2024), "Safeguarding Charities Act"; online at https://www.congress.gov/bill/118th-congress/senate-bill/3604/related-bills.

[21] National Conference of State Legislatures, "Education Legislation: Bill Tracking" (current as of June 11, 2024); online at https://tinyurl.com/yb58rdvf. Movement Advancement Project, "LGBTQ Curricular Laws" (interactive); online at https://www.lgbtmap.org/equality-maps/curricular_laws. Hannah Natanson, Lauren Tierney, and Clara Ence Morse, "Which States Are Restricting, or Requiring, Lessons on Race, Sex and Gender," *The Washington Post*, April 4, 2024; online at https://www.washingtonpost.com/education/2024/education-laws-states-teaching-race-gender-sex/. Kiara Alfonseca, "Map: The Impact of Anti-DEI Legislation," ABC News, May 5, 2024; online at https://abcnews.go.com/US/map-impact-anti-dei-legislation/story?id=108795967. Bella DiMarco, "Legislative Tracker: 2023 Parent-Rights Bills in the States," FutureEd, March 16, 2023; online at https://www.future-ed.org/legislative-tracker-2023-parent-rights-bills-in-the-states/.

[22] Georgia General Assembly, "Parents and Children Protection Act of 2023"; online at https://www.legis.ga.gov/legislation/63991. This bill would have required *all* schools—public and private—to provide parental notification before teaching about gender identity and prohibited schools from noting a change in a student's gender identity without parental consent. It was not acted upon. In April 2024, the Idaho legislature passed House Bill 710, which requires public and private schools as well as public libraries to remove materials deemed harmful to children or face lawsuits; online at https://legislature.idaho.gov/wp-content/uploads/sessioninfo/2024/legislation/H0710E1.pdf.

[23] U.S. Department of Education, "U.S. Department of Education Releases Final Title IX Regulations, Providing Vital Protections Against Sex Discrimination," April 19, 2024; online at https://tinyurl.com/4r64x39y.

[24] The House passed a Parental Bill of Rights in 2023, but the Senate did not act on the legislation. H.R. 5, 118th Congress (2023-2024), "Parents Bill of Rights"; online at https://www.congress.gov/bill/118th-congress/house-bill/5/text.

[25] S. 2938, 117th Congress (2022-2023), "Bipartisan Safer Communities Act"; online at https://www.congress.gov/bill/117th-congress/senate-bill/2938/text.

[26] Jamiel Lynch, "Should Teachers Be Armed? Tennessee Passes Bill That Would Allow School Staff to Carry Concealed Gun," ABC Eyewitness News, April 24, 2024; online at https://tinyurl.com/5dfex8de.

[27] Bipartisan Policy Center, "State Paid Family Leave Laws Across the U.S.," January 16, 2024; online at https://bipartisanpolicy.org/explainer/state-paid-family-leave-laws-across-the-u-s/. Kathryn Mayer, "Access to Paid Family Leave Climbed in 2023," SHRM, September 21, 2023; online at https://www.shrm.org/topics-tools/news/benefits-compensation/access-to-paid-family-leave-climbed-2023. Mike Ramsey, "Emerging Trends in Paid Leave Offer New Support for Employees," SHRM, September 15, 2023; online at https://www.shrm.org/topics-tools/news/all-things-work/expanding-view-paid-leave. American Fidelity, "2024 Paid Leave Trends," December 19, 2023; online at https://americanfidelity.com/blog/general/2024-paid-leave-trends/.

[28] FordHarrison LLP, "District of Columbia Joins Trend Toward Greater Pay Transparency," January 19, 2024; online at https://www.fordharrison.com/district-of-columbia-joins-trend-

toward-to-greater-pay-transparency. Alyssa Lankford, "Pay Transparency Laws the Latest Trend in Advancing Goal of Pay Equity," McAfee & Taft, August 22, 2023; online at https://www.mcafeetaft.com/pay-transparency-laws-the-latest-trend-in-advancing-goal-of-pay-equity/.

[29] "Children's Online Privacy Protection Rule," *Federal Register*, January 11, 2024; online at https://tinyurl.com/bdf4me4m. In June 2024, a new draft of the federal privacy law, the American Privacy Rights Act, was released. See Jedidiah Bracy, "New Draft APRA Released Ahead of 27 June Markup," IAPP, June 21, 2024; online at https://iapp.org/news/a/new-draft-apra-released-ahead-of-27-june-markup.

4

The Student Experience Forecast

By Morva McDonald and Debra P. Wilson

Morva McDonald is vice president of leadership and governance at NAIS.

Debra P. Wilson is president of NAIS.

Key Takeaways

- Persistent impacts from the pandemic, along with other external cultural factors, are having significant effects on students' mental health and well-being.
- Schools and public officials are increasingly focused on the influence of social media and cellphone use on young people.
- As the need to address students' mental health concerns gains more widespread acceptance, schools are being called on to address the unique challenges of specific groups—including boys, Black students, and students who identify as LGBTQ+.

The Pandemic and Other Cultural Forces Continue to Affect Students' Mental Health and Well-Being

The COVID-19 pandemic significantly impacted the student experience in and beyond school. While comprehensive research is not yet available on the pandemic's long-term influence on social-emotional development, findings from school research and developmental psychology point to opportunities for deepening student support.

Beyond learning losses, the disruptions and instability of the pandemic caused some children to miss key opportunities to learn skills associated with developmental milestones. For example, babies born during the pandemic had significantly lower scores at 6 months of age on "gross motor, fine motor, and personal-social subdomains" compared with babies born before the pandemic.[1] Among school-age children, anxiety and depression rose precipitously during the pandemic, along with increased rates of ADHD, obsessive-compulsive disorder, and tics. Children ages 6 to 12 were more emotionally dysregulated (e.g., had marked fluctuations in mood and mood swings), and they exhibited more "internalizing" issues (e.g., withdrawal, low self-esteem, eating disturbances) and "externalizing" behaviors (e.g., agitation, conduct problems) compared to pre-pandemic rates.[2]

For some teens, the stress of the pandemic (in the world and in their own homes) threatened to interrupt a few specific developmental stages. For example, typically, teens have to first feel stable in order to "individuate" from their parents, to take risks, and to begin to self-regulate their emotions. The pandemic threatened such feelings of stability.[3] Beyond the pandemic, coexistent external stressors—from existential threats like gun violence, climate change, and polarization, to complex global conflicts—have compounded stressors for many children.

The deterioration in some students' social-emotional well-being during the pandemic showed up in different ways in classrooms of all school types. In May 2022, more than eight in 10 public elementary school teachers said they had seen delayed behavioral and social-emotional development in their students because of the pandemic. Further, 83% agreed or strongly agreed that it had negatively impacted behavioral development, and 87% agreed or strongly agreed that it had impacted social-emotional development.[4] In independent schools, 63% of elementary school teachers responding to a November 2023 NAIS Snapshot Survey and 52% of all teachers reported seeing an increase in behavioral issues among students.[5]

Beyond managing these additional challenges in the classroom, teachers have had to reset their expectations and rethink the strategies they use to scaffold learning and student support. The focus on the whole child has long been a mainstay of educational theories and practices. But, increasingly, researchers and practitioners are revitalizing their commitments to social-emotional learning (SEL) within the core curriculum to better support children as they navigate multiple stressors. Indeed, there is growing consensus among researchers that social and emotional skills are essential to learning and life outcomes.[6] Although SEL has been the focus of recent political debate, most NAIS schools have long incorporated elements of SEL (even if under a different name) in their curriculum and programming, and most parents want their children to learn these skills.[7]

Schools and Public Leaders Are Focusing on the Impact on Young People of Social Media and Cellphone Use

Other external factors that are drawing attention include social media and cellphone use in schools.

Specifically, some researchers are raising concerns about the social-emotional and developmental effects of social media use. For example, one much-talked-about recent book is Jonathan Haidt's *The Anxious Generation: How the Great Rewiring of Childhood Is Causing an Epidemic of Mental Illness*. Haidt argues that social media use, paired with a longer-growing trend of overparenting and the loss of self-directed play, has significantly impacted social-emotional development in young people. In particular, he calls out concerns about increasing social anxiety and depression among girls and increasing social isolation and disengagement among boys.[8] It's important to note that other researchers have questioned the degree of causality between social media and mental health distress,[9] and indeed, this is an area still being closely studied.

The emerging research about the link between technology use and youth mental health is leading some federal, state, and local governing bodies to take policy, legal, and legislative action. In 2021, the U.S. Surgeon General warned of the link between social media use and the rise in depression, anxiety, and suicide among young people.[10] In June 2024, he called for warning labels on social media.[11] In addition to the U.S. Senate hearings with social media companies, states are also addressing this issue, introducing dozens of bills to limit young people's use of particular sites and apps. Some of these laws are going into effect, while some are being blocked in courts, mostly on the grounds of First Amendment violations.[12]

Cellphone use by young people is also a cause of concern. Nearly three-fourths, or 72%, of U.S. high school teachers say cellphone distraction is a major problem in the classroom.[13] In an effort to protect students' well-being and respond to teachers' needs, a few major public school districts, from New York City to Los Angeles County, have banned or are making moves to ban cellphone use in schools. Florida was the first state to move to ban cellphone use in K-12 classrooms, and as of summer 2024, nine other states are considering such a bill.[14]

Independent schools, too, are exploring options for programs and policies related to cellphones. For example, in a May 2024 NAIS Snapshot Survey, 93% of respondents reported that their school regulated or prohibited student cellphone use on school grounds or in classrooms in some way. However, only 7% indicated that their students are not allowed to bring phones to school at all.[15]

Research Indicates That Some Students Are Especially Vulnerable to Mental Health Risks

Beyond providing healthy environments for all students, school leaders and educators play an important role in identifying and supporting individual students and subpopulations of students vulnerable to mental health risk. While all subpopulations of students have concerns worthy of attention, in this section we'll look at three in particular: male students, Black students, and students within the LGBTQ+ community.

Male Students

Increasingly, both research and experience indicate that boys and young men are struggling with mental health.

In the area of academic outcomes, gender gaps persist on many levels. Across the U.S., fewer boys are graduating from high school,[16] enrollment in college is down by a greater amount among males than females,[17] and there's a widening gender gap in college completion.[18] In independent schools, the NAIS High School Survey of Student Engagement (HSSSE) showed differences by gender in academic motivation: Only 30% of boys said they were motivated by a desire to get good grades (compared to 60% of girls) and 18% by a desire to learn (compared to 28% of girls).[19]

Beyond academics, recent research reveals concerns related to boys' mental health. In 2020 the American Psychological Association created the Task Force on Boys in School to study the challenges male students face and develop fact sheets that can "inform decisions at all levels of the U.S. educational system." So far, the Task Force has released several peer-reviewed fact sheets on subjects such as "Exploring Boys' (Mis)Behavior," "Learning Disabilities," and "High-Achieving Boys."[20]

Risk of suicide and suicidal ideation is on the rise for boys. In 2021, nearly four times as many males died by suicide as females, according to the CDC, and suicides among male teens and young men in particular have shown a massive increase.[21]

One possible explanation for the increase in suicide is the societal expectations affecting boys' well-being and emotional expression. Societal factors are also what Ruth Whippman, author of *BoyMom: Reimagining Boyhood in the Age of Impossible Masculinity*, points to as a major factor in what she calls an epidemic of loneliness among boys and young men. She cites a survey reporting that more than a quarter of men under 30 say they have no close friends; further, teenage boys spend two hours fewer a week socializing than girls (and seven more per week on screens). Whippman argues that old problems (notably, boys being socialized in different ways and inadequately taught emotional expression) are colliding with a new one—wider cultural reckoning about toxic masculinity.[22]

Some experts suggest that mental health concerns in boys can sometimes go undetected because the symptoms look different than they do for girls. For example, some boys may show irritability, frustration, and aggression rather than more traditionally recognized signs of depression, such as melancholy. In addition, data show that some young males stopped engaging in mental health support during the pandemic; while antidepressant prescriptions rose dramatically for teenage girls and women in their 20s, for young men they declined abruptly during March 2020 and did not recover. Research indicates that, rather than having recovered, the young men simply stopped taking the medication they needed.[23]

Black Students

As a group, Black students are also experiencing elevated challenges with mental health and well-being. This is a significant problem with a complex and longstanding context. Black students have historically faced persistent levels of marginalization within and outside of education, and many of today's external stressors have disproportionately impacted Black students and other students of color.

As is true with boys, suicide is an area of concern. Suicide rates among Black youth in the U.S. are growing at an exponential rate. For instance, from 2018 to 2021, Black children and young adults had the largest increase in suicide rates among 10- to 24-year-olds, at 37%.[24] This increase came on top of the already alarming reality that Black youth in the period between 2000 and 2020 experienced a 78% increase in suicides.[25] Further, Black children ages 5 to 12 were found to be two times more likely to die by suicide than their white counterparts.[26] Finally, children who experience racial discrimination, as so many Black youth do, are more than three times more likely to have suicidal thoughts, make a suicide plan, and attempt suicide than those who do not.[27]

Feelings about belonging may factor in for Black students. A recent analysis of data from the Independent School Health Check found that, on average, 83% of students in independent schools agreed with the statement "I feel like I belong at this school." However, when these data are disaggregated by race, only 74% of Black students agreed.[28] This finding on its own does not suggest a significant challenge. But when it is considered in conjunction with the increase in the mental health issues facing Black students, it becomes clear that independent schools have a significant opportunity to improve the experience of these students.

LGBTQ+ Students

LGBTQ+ students are also experiencing worse mental health, as a group, than their non-LGBTQ+ peers. Despite greater visibility and social acceptance for LGBTQ+ students than in the past, they have significantly higher rates of anxiety, depression, and suicidal thoughts than their non-LGBTQ+ peers.[29]

Suicide is also an issue for this subpopulation of students. According to the CDC, LGBTQ+ young people are more than four times as likely to attempt suicide as their peers. The Trevor Project's "2023 U.S National Survey of the Mental Health of LGBTQ Young People" found that 41% of the respondents had seriously considered attempting suicide in the past year, including roughly half of transgender and nonbinary youth.[30]

The Trevor Project's research consistently points to key protective factors for LGBTQ+ students, including connection to supportive, trusted adults and friends as well as safe spaces and inclusive activities.[31] While many independent schools have a positive track record when it comes to supporting their LGBTQ+ students, it is still an area of concern. NAIS researcher Margaret Anne Rowe writes in an advisory:

> In a 2021 survey, the LGBTQ+ youth organization GLSEN found that students in private schools, including independent schools, heard fewer anti-LGBTQ+ remarks at school, felt supported by greater numbers of staff members, and were more likely to have access to LGBTQ+-related resources and supports on campus than students in public schools. At the same time, LGBTQ+ students in independent schools often aren't doing as well as their non-LGBTQ+ peers when it comes to their mental and physical health. Though nearly 75% of non-LGBTQ+ students described their health as "very good" or "excellent," only 53% of LGBTQ+ students, and 42% of transgender and nonbinary students, said the same.[32]

Schools of all types, including independent schools, face the tremendous challenge of caring for children and young people in the context of a broad collection of external stressors—from the pandemic, to social media ubiquity, to complex global conflicts, to existential threats like climate change and gun violence. In addition, the increase in political and cultural polarization within the United States has led to increases in hate speech and hate crimes against some of the most vulnerable students, significantly impacting their health and well-being. Schools that bolster their mental health services, their curriculum for social-emotional learning and well-being, and their policies and practices will be best positioned to support each and every student in their care.

QUESTIONS TO ASK

- How is your school preparing and supporting teachers so they can identify students with mental health challenges or social-emotional learning needs? How might your school educate and partner with parents to provide wraparound care for students?
- In what ways does your school use research focused on the impact of social media and cellphone use on students' health and well-being to inform policies, curricular decisions, professional development for teachers, and education for families?
- What does your school's data reveal about the differential experience of students, particularly those who are part of a marginalized group? In what ways could your school better understand the realities and needs of specific groups of students? How can your leadership team, faculty, staff, and families deepen the support and resources they provide students?

STEPS TO TAKE

- Provide teachers with information on developmental milestones and encourage them to brainstorm ways to help children grow toward these milestones.
- Support teachers with opportunities to refine their pedagogical practices to better address the needs of students.
- Explore policies and practices related to social media use that reflect the school's and community's mission, vision, and values as well as current knowledge and research.
- For subpopulations of concern, analyze the data available. Your school can participate in the Independent School Health Check survey, for example, or the NAIS Assessment of Inclusivity and Multiculturalism.
- Connection to supportive adults and friends is consistently identified in research as a protective factor in students' overall well-being. Evaluate the protective factors at your school for subpopulations at risk;

for example, assess the degree to which individual students have a trusting adult they can count on. In addition, identify national and local resources to support students experiencing suicidal ideation.

MORE TO EXPLORE

Access further information here.

"2023 U.S. National Survey of the Mental Health of LGBTQ Young People," The Trevor Project:
https://www.thetrevorproject.org/survey-2023/assets/static/05_TREVOR05_2023survey.pdf

***The Anxious Generation: How the Great Rewiring of Childhood Is Causing an Epidemic of Mental Illness*, Jonathan Haidt**

***BoyMom: Reimagining Boyhood in the Age of Impossible Masculinity*, Ruth Whippman**

"Helping Boys Deal with Loneliness," Ray Swann, *Psychology Today*:
https://www.psychologytoday.com/us/blog/raising-healthy-boys/202401/helping-boys-deal-with-loneliness

High School Survey of Student Engagement (HSSSE) and Middle Grades Survey of Student Engagement (MGSSE):
https://www.nais.org/analyze/student-engagement-surveys/

Independent School Health Check (ISHC), NAIS:
https://www.nais.org/analyze/independent-school-health-check/

NAIS Assessment of Inclusivity and Multiculturalism (AIM):
https://nais.org/analyze/assessment-of-inclusivity-and-multiculturalism/

"NAIS Research on LGBTQ+ Youth Well-Being: Part 1: The State of LGBTQ+ Youth," Margaret Anne Rowe, NAIS:
https://www.nais.org/articles/pages/member/research/nais-research-on-lgbtq-youth-well-being-chapter-1/#_edn1/

"NAIS Research on LGBTQ+ Youth Well-Being: Part 2: LGBTQ+ Students and the Independent School Health Check," Margaret Anne Rowe, NAIS:

https://www.nais.org/articles/pages/member/research/nais-research-on-lgbtq-youth-well-being-part-2-independent-school-health-check-data/

"Trends in Grades, Academic Pressure, and Belonging by Race," Phillip Brooks, NAIS:
https://www.nais.org/articles/pages/member/research/nais-research-advisory-trends-in-grades-academic-pressure-and-belonging-by-race/

ENDNOTES

[1] Lauren C. Shuffrey et al., "Association of Birth During the COVID-19 Pandemic with Neurodevelopmental Status at 6 Months in Infants with and Without In Utero Exposure to Maternal SARS-CoV-2 Infection," *JAMA Pediatrics*, January 4, 2022; online at https://jamanetwork.com/journals/jamapediatrics/fullarticle/2787479.

[2] Tumaini Rucker Coker, Jennifer Appleton Gootman, and Emily P. Backes, eds., *Addressing the Long-Term Effects of the COVID-19 Pandemic on Children and Families* (Washington, DC: The National Academies of Sciences, Engineering, and Medicine, 2023); online at https://nap.nationalacademies.org/catalog/26809/addressing-the-long-term-effects-of-the-covid-19-pandemic-on-children-and-families.

[3] Diana Divecha, "Recovering from the Pandemic: What's the New Normal for Teens and How Can We Help?" *Developmental Science* blog, June 27, 2023; online at https://www.developmentalscience.com/blog/2023/6/15/recovering-from-the-pandemic.

[4] U.S. Department of Education, Institute of Education Sciences, "School Pulse Panel: Back to School Responses to COVID-19," 2021-2022; online at https://ies.ed.gov/schoolsurvey/spp/.

[5] NAIS Snapshot Survey, "Teacher Retention at a Glance," November 17 to December 5, 2023; online at https://www.nais.org/getmedia/1bfba474-5d98-4708-b6fa-3d662e39d33f/NAIS-Research_Snapshot-Survey-Teacher-Wellbeing_12-8-23.pdf.

[6] Stephanie M. Jones et al., *Navigating SEL from the Inside Out: Looking Inside & Across Leading SEL Programs: A Practical Resource for Schools and OT Providers* (New York: Wallace Foundation/EASEL Lab, Harvard Graduate School of Education, 2022); online at https://wallacefoundation.org/sites/default/files/2023-09/navigating-social-and-emotional-learning-from-the-inside-out-middle-high-school.pdf.

[7] The Education Trust, "Why America's Students Need Social and Emotional Learning Now, More Than Ever," March 10, 2023; online at https://tinyurl.com/mu4453jx.

[8] Jonathan Haidt, *The Anxious Generation: How the Great Rewiring of Childhood Is Causing an Epidemic of Mental Illness* (New York: Penguin Press, 2024).

[9] Candice L. Odgers, "The Great Rewiring: Is Social Media Really Behind an Epidemic of Teenage Mental Illness?" *Nature*, March 29, 2024; online at https://www.nature.com/articles/d41586-024-00902-2.

[10] Vivek H. Murthy, *Protecting Youth Mental Health: The U.S. Surgeon General's Advisory* (Washington, DC: U.S. Public Health Service, 2021); online at https://www.hhs.gov/sites/default/files/surgeon-general-youth-mental-health-advisory.pdf.

[11] Vivek H. Murthy, "Surgeon General: Why I'm Calling for a Warning Label on Social Media Platforms," *The New York Times*, June 17, 2024; online at https://www.nytimes.com/2024/06/17/opinion/social-media-health-warning.html.

[12] Jason Kelley and Aaron Mackey, "States Attack Young People's Constitutional Right to Use

Social Media: 2023 Year in Review," Electronic Frontier Foundation, December 30, 2023; online at https://www.eff.org/deeplinks/2023/12/states-attack-young-peoples-constitutional-right-use-social-media-2023-year-review.

[13] Jenn Hatfield, "72% of U.S. High School Teachers Say Cellphone Distraction Is a Major Problem in the Classroom," Pew Research Center, June 12, 2024; online at https://tinyurl.com/5dac9t2j.

[14] Arianna Prothero, "States Are Cracking Down on Cellphones in Schools. What That Looks Like," *Education Week*, May 23, 2024 (corr. June 26, 2024); online at https://www.edweek.org/technology/states-are-cracking-down-on-cellphones-in-schools-what-that-looks-like/2024/05.

[15] NAIS Snapshot Survey, "Phone Regulation at a Glance," May 6-8, 2024; online at https://www.nais.org/getmedia/390cf955-e9a7-4f9f-b55e-361bb0895206/NAISsnapshotSurveyPhoneReg051024.pdf.

[16] Richard V. Reeves and Simran Kalkat, "Racial Disparities in the High School Graduation Gender Gap," Brookings Institution, April 18, 2023; online at https://www.brookings.edu/articles/racial-disparities-in-the-high-school-graduation-gender-gap/.

[17] National Center for Education Statistics, "Actual and Projected Undergraduate Enrollment in Degree-Granting Postsecondary Institutions, by Sex, Fall 2010 Through Fall 2031," Fast Facts; online at https://nces.ed.gov/fastfacts/display.asp?id=98.

[18] Richard V. Reeves and Ember Smith, "The Male College Crisis Is Not Just in Enrollment, But in Completion," Brookings Institution, October 8, 2021; online at https://www.brookings.edu/articles/the-male-college-crisis-is-not-just-in-enrollment-but-completion/.

[19] Grant Stringer, "Trends in the 2023 High School Survey of Student Engagement (HSSSE)," NAIS, Fall 2023; online at https://www.nais.org/getmedia/8fa2b01c-2f75-44fb-97a0-215e951c4917/NAIS-Research_Fall-2023-HSSSE-Report_2-2024.pdf.

[20] Zara Abrams, "Boys Are Facing Key Challenges in School. Inside the Effort to Support Their Success," *Monitor on Psychology*, April/May 2023; online at https://www.apa.org/monitor/2023/04/boys-school-challenges-recommendations.

[21] Sally C. Curtin, Matthew F. Garnett, and Farida B. Ahmad, "Provisional Numbers and Rates of Suicide by Month and Demographic Characteristics: United States, 2021," *Vital Statistics Rapid Release*, September 2022; online at https://www.cdc.gov/nchs/data/vsrr/vsrr024.pdf.

[22] Ruth Whippman, "Boys Get Everything, Except the Thing That's Most Worth Having," *The New York Times*, June 5, 2024; online at https://www.nytimes.com/2024/06/05/opinion/boys-parenting-loneliness.html. Statistics from a survey by American Enterprise Institute in May 2021 (Daniel A. Cox, "Men's Social Circles Are Shrinking," Survey Center on American Life, June 29, 2021; online at https://www.americansurveycenter.org/why-mens-social-circles-are-shrinking/).

[23] Erika Edwards, "'Boys Are Disappearing' from Mental Health Care as Signs of Depression Go Undetected," NBC News, March 17, 2024; online at https://www.nbcnews.com/health/health-news/depression-anxiety-teen-boys-diagnosis-undetected-rcna141649. Kao-Ping Chua et al., "Antidepressant Dispensing to US Adolescents and Young Adults: 2016-2022," *Pediatrics*, February 26, 2024; online at https://publications.aap.org/pediatrics/article/153/3/e2023064245/196655/Antidepressant-Dispensing-to-US-Adolescents-and?autologincheck=redirected.

[24] Deborah M. Stone, Karin A. Mack, and Judith Qualters, "Notes from the Field: Recent Changes in Suicide Rates, by Race and Ethnicity and Age Group—United States, 2021," *Morbidity and Mortality Weekly Report*, February 10, 2023; online at https://www.cdc.gov/mmwr/volumes/72/wr/mm7206a4.htm?s_cid=mm7206a4_w#suggestedcitation.

[25] U.S. Centers for Disease Control and Prevention, "Underlying Cause of Death: 2018-2022"; online at https://wonder.cdc.gov/ucd-icd10.html.

[26] Jeffrey A. Bridges et al., "Age-Related Racial Disparity in Suicide Rates Among US Youths from 2001 Through 2015," *JAMA Pediatrics*, May 21, 2018; online at https://www.ncbi.nlm.nih.gov/pmc/articles/PMC6137506/.

[27] Philip Baiden et al., "Perceived Racial Discrimination and Suicide Behaviors Among Racial and Ethnic Minority Adolescents in the United States: Findings from the 2021 Adolescent Behaviors and Experiences Survey," *Psychiatry Research*, November 2022; online at https://pubmed.ncbi.nlm.nih.gov/36244159/.

[28] Phillip Brooks, "Trends in Grades, Academic Pressure, and Belonging by Race," NAIS, November 29, 2023; online at https://www.nais.org/articles/pages/member/research/nais-research-advisory-trends-in-grades-academic-pressure-and-belonging-by-race/.

[29] Margaret Anne Rowe, "NAIS Research on LGBTQ+ Youth Well-Being: Part 1: The State of LGBTQ+ Youth," NAIS, November 2023; online at https://www.nais.org/articles/pages/member/research/nais-research-on-lgbtq-youth-well-being-chapter-1/#_edn1.

[30] The Trevor Project, "Facts About Suicide Among LGBTQ+ Young People," January 1, 2024; online at https://www.thetrevorproject.org/resources/article/facts-about-lgbtq-youth-suicide/; and "2023 U.S. National Survey of the Mental Health of LGBTQ Young People," 2023; online at https://www.thetrevorproject.org/survey-2023/assets/static/05_TREVOR05_2023survey.pdf.

[31] Ibid.

[32] Margaret Anne Rowe, "NAIS Research on LGBTQ+ Youth Well-Being: Part 2: LGBTQ+ Students and the Independent School Health Check," NAIS, April 2024; online at https://www.nais.org/articles/pages/member/research/nais-research-on-lgbtq-youth-well-being-part-2-independent-school-health-check-data/.

5

The Equity and Justice Forecast

By Caroline G. Blackwell, Morva McDonald, and Myra McGovern

Caroline G. Blackwell is vice president of equity and justice initiatives at NAIS.

Morva McDonald is vice president of leadership and governance.

Myra McGovern is vice president of external affairs.

Key Takeaways

- Two NAIS surveys, one of diversity practitioners and the other about governing boards, show that the scope of schools' diversity, equity, and inclusion (DEI) efforts has grown. But to keep up with future needs, more operating support and commitment will be required at the leadership level.
- As polarization in the United States increases, so will the need for both schools and their DEI staffs to work within a contentious atmosphere and effectively manage the acrimony that has become more common.
- Like some businesses, some educational institutions that face criticism of their DEI efforts are deciding to rebrand or rethink their approach to the work.

DEI Work Has Grown, But Inadequate Infrastructure and Resources Make It Challenging to Meet Future Needs

Diversity, equity, and inclusion work has been important to many independent schools' missions, visions, and values for decades. Since the 1960s, the focus of DEI efforts has evolved to stay in step with broader social, political, cultural, and education trends. In the 2020s, the work has continued to grow, tackling some of the most challenging issues communities face.

But too often, resources and infrastructure have failed to keep pace. Many sectors, and many DEI practitioners, would benefit if the scope of DEI work were better articulated and defined. In the current context, scope creep, small budgets, and unclear goals, along with internal and external pressures, are likely to compound the challenges facing DEI commitments within independent schools.

In the 1960s and 1970s, many independent schools sought to recruit students of color, and some created Offices for Minority Student Affairs. In the 1980s and 1990s, recognizing that socioeconomic status also posed a great barrier to equal access, some schools expanded their programs to address social class and income disparities as well as race and ethnicity.

The 1980s and 1990s also ushered in an awareness that students performed better when they saw themselves represented among the topics they were studying. Schools often renamed their departments to indicate a focus on multicultural education.

In the early 2000s, many offices worked to address the disparate impacts of discrimination on some students. By this time, DEI offices were also engaged in examining and ameliorating the adverse outcomes of structural and systemic power dynamics on equality and equity of access, opportunity, and teaching and learning outcomes. Diversity offices at schools and colleges sought to celebrate difference and help ensure that students had equal opportunities to benefit from education. Later, building community and ensuring that all students were included and experienced a sense of belonging also became part of this work.

Now, the work of diversity, equity, and inclusion includes a broad range of responsibilities and activities at many schools. These often include a focus on organizational policies and practices—everything from developing policies aimed at ensuring equitable compensation to adopting practices focused on

TABLE 1

DEI Duties Range Broadly from Planning Programming to Managing Conflict

PERCENTAGE OF RESPONDENTS WHOSE JOBS INCLUDED EACH RESPONSIBILITY

Planning diversity programs/overseeing diversity programming	93%
Consulting with faculty/administrators on diversity-related problems or incidents	89%
Interacting with other administrators on diversity initiatives	88%
Presenting/conducting workshops on diversity topics	86%
Supporting teacher-led DEI and multicultural education	83%
Conducting workshops on diversity topics	82%
Developing, monitoring strategic diversity/inclusion plan	82%
Supporting all school groups that fall within the diversity umbrella	80%
Meeting regularly with the head of school to report on diversity	78%
Training faculty/staff/parents/students/alumni	78%
Teaching about diversity	75%
Conducting/assisting with new faculty orientation on diversity-related topics	74%
Supporting hiring policies and practices to ensure a diverse workforce	73%
Serving as adviser to DEI-related student clubs and programs	73%
Reporting to the board on diversity initiatives	73%
Internal DEI data collection and reporting	71%
Monitoring policy and regulatory changes related to diversity issues	71%
Managing budgets	67%
Serving on the school's diversity committee/council	67%
Conflict intervention and management among/between students	65%
Curriculum review/development	64%
Recruiting faculty/staff from underrepresented racial, ethnic, and cultural backgrounds	62%
Serving on the board's diversity committee/council	56%
External relations liaison	53%
Acting as a liaison in the admissions process	53%
Conflict intervention and management among/between faculty and staff	52%
Leading and/or supporting community outreach	47%
Recruiting students from underrepresented racial, ethnic, and cultural backgrounds	41%
Planning, supporting global education programs/initiatives	30%

Source: Phillip Brooks, "2023-2024 State of Independent School Diversity Practice," NAIS

FIGURE 1

The Majority of Schools Have Had a Diversity Director for Five Years or Fewer

NUMBER OF YEARS SCHOOLS REPORT HAVING A DIVERSITY DIRECTOR

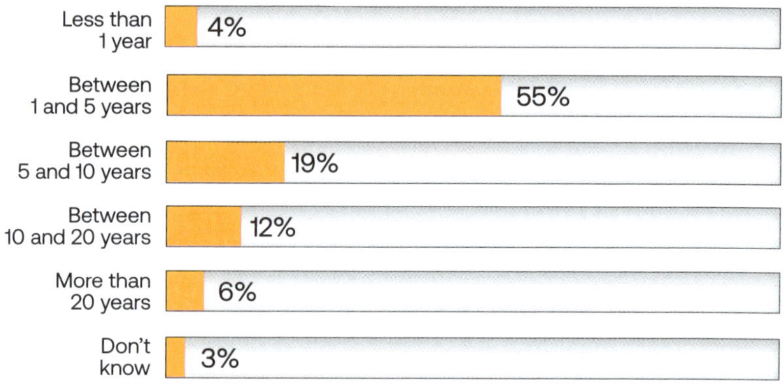

Source: Phillip Brooks, "2023-2024 State of Independent School Diversity Practice," NAIS

supporting the faculty's sense of belonging. At the same time, DEI efforts often extend into equity and inclusion within teaching and learning, including curricular decisions and practices related to participation in classrooms.

Just how much the work has expanded is substantiated by DEI practitioners, who take on a broad range of responsibilities. Nearly 90% of the practitioners who responded to NAIS's Diversity Practitioner Survey said that they regularly consulted with faculty or administration on diversity-related problems or incidents. Eighty-six percent presented or conducted workshops on diversity topics. Significantly fewer recruited students from underrepresented groups (41%) or planned global education programming (30%) (Table 1).[1]

Fifty-five percent of respondents to the survey said that their school had had a diversity director for between one and five years, while 37% reported that their school had had this role for more than five years (Figure 1).[2]

Seventy-five percent of survey respondents fulfill their practitioner duties on a full-time basis. In 2019, only 54% of respondents did so.[3]

Asked how well their responsibilities are spelled out, 40% of respondents said their work was extremely or very well-defined. But 20% reported that their duties were either not well-defined (17%) or not defined at all (3%) (Figure 2).[4]

FIGURE 2

Diversity Practitioners Have Differing Perceptions of How Clear Their Duties Are

HOW DIVERSITY PRACTITIONERS DESCRIBE THEIR RESPONSIBILITIES

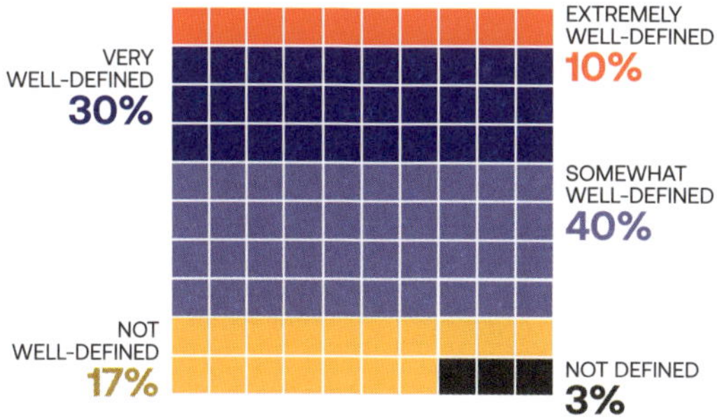

Source: Phillip Brooks, "2023-2024 State of Independent School Diversity Practice," NAIS

For many schools, infrastructure and resources to accomplish diversity work are also lacking. Slightly less than 50% of all respondents reported that their school had a strategic diversity plan. In addition, schools varied in budget allocations for diversity work. Twenty-one percent of schools reported having more than $50,000 budgeted for diversity initiatives, but another 21% reported having $5,000 or less per year (9%) or no budget at all (12%).[5]

Another area of infrastructure challenge can be seen in the uneven distribution of institutional policy supporting DEI work.

According to NAIS's *2023-2024 State of Independent School Governance*, fewer than a third of schools have permanent DEI board committees. Fifty-five percent of school leaders responding to the NAIS Governance Survey reported having an approved written DEI policy.[6]

Some DEI practitioners have expressed frustration that their work has grown in scope and complexity, yet budgets and staffing have failed to keep pace. Similarly, while 77% of practitioners reported receiving a good deal or a great deal of support from their head of school, only 35% of practitioners reported that board members were similarly supportive.[7]

Without stronger leadership support and a better articulation of the goals and responsibilities for diversity work, practitioners are likely to burn out. To maintain momentum for the work, schools will need to clarify their DEI goals and devote appropriate resources to achieving them.

External Pressures Are Causing Contention for Some DEI Offices

In addition to the challenge of being responsible for a broad range of initiatives with few resources, growing polarization and animus related to the 2024 presidential election are affecting the role of the DEI practitioner—as they are affecting all facets of life in the United States. When political strategists redefined and weaponized "critical race theory" as a wedge tool in early 2021, many DEI offices at schools and colleges had to devote significant time to refuting false claims about their work and navigating an increasing partisan divide. Many topics and practices common in schools—such as helping students manage conflict, teaching the history of chattel slavery in the United States, or using social-emotional learning to help students understand their feelings—were attacked as divisive or labeled "indoctrination."[8]

As DEI became the focus of partisan contention, many DEI practitioners became more knowledgeable about polarization. Polarization itself then became a topic for practitioners to manage, ironically generating additional negative attention to DEI work.

Asked to describe U.S. politics in one word, most respondents to a Pew poll chose "divisive."

In the August 2023 NAIS Hot Issues Survey, 97% of heads reported that "responding to conflict in and about independent schools" was one of the top challenges they were facing. The survey report described the conundrum facing school leaders: Increasingly, parents' views on issues such as diversity, equity, and inclusion are highly polarized, and "any attempts to address the concerns of one group will provoke the other, and doing nothing will bring continued criticism from both groups of parents."[9]

As election season now extends longer than in the past, and factious rhetoric and vitriol are more constant, many Americans are frustrated with the political system and, increasingly, with other members of their community. When respondents in a Pew Research poll were asked to describe politics in the United States in a single word or phrase, "divisive" (or variations of it, such as "divided") was the word most often chosen. Seventy-nine percent of respondents to this question expressed a negative sentiment. Nearly two-thirds said that they felt exhausted when thinking about politics, and more than half (55%) reported feeling angry.[10]

This divisiveness is also undermining community bonds, according to Gallup. A survey found that people who lived in communities where the dominant political sentiment differed from their own views were less likely to report that they felt attached to their community. And while 66% of Americans reported that most people in their area can be trusted, "one's perceptions of their community's ideological leaning influences how much people trust their fellow residents."[11]

Many people working in independent schools are worried about the impact of this political climate on students, faculty, and the school community as a whole. Dealing with school families who are upset with some aspect of the school's programming can take up a significant amount of teacher and administrator time. Occasionally, families who are dissatisfied create a toxic environment for others, and that toxicity creates frustration for faculty and may even lead teachers to leave the profession.[12]

Across the county, schools are working to provide guidelines for how to teach in ways that encourage classroom dialogue and allow students to express their opinions without feeling social pressure to adhere to a particular viewpoint. One group of school leaders, led by Deerfield Academy Head of School John Austin, created a framework by which schools can better serve populations that represent a range of values and beliefs. *Thriving in a World of Pluralistic Contention: A Framework for Schools*, funded by the Edward E. Ford Foundation, seeks to guide teachers and protect schools from outside attacks.[13]

When political or issue polarization manifests within the student body, schools are forced to define what constitutes acceptable speech. While public school students have certain free speech rights, independent schools that do not accept federal financial assistance can institute speech policies and declare when and where protests can or cannot take place unless the state where the school is located provides protection. Many schools are bracing for periods of greater contention by practicing tabletop exercises to plan what they would do in a variety of situations.

For many independent schools, clearer articulation of DEI work and its role in meeting the school's unique mission is needed. Without clear goals, explicit leadership and support from their heads of school and board, and an achievable scope of work, DEI offices can flounder.

In the Face of Larger Sociopolitical Pressures, Some Organizations Beyond Education Will Continue to Reconceptualize the Work of DEI

Schools are not alone in managing increasing polarization while trying to reach organizational goals for equity and inclusion. Many businesses have also had to juggle the needs of constituent groups—including consumers, shareholders, boards, and employees—and their business objectives.

A *New York Times* article credits the 2023 Supreme Court ruling about affirmative action for "setting off a wave of similar lawsuits and legal threats against company diversity programs." The article describes companies' moves to rebrand DEI, such as referring to a survey that might have once been called a DEI survey as a "culture survey" or focusing on the desired outcomes of a training (e.g., helping managers deliver performance reviews more effectively), rather than the content.[14]

Universities, too, have faced increasing backlash against diversity work, and some state legislatures have even banned DEI programming in public institutions. *The Chronicle of Higher Education* tracks this legislation and reported that 85 bills have been introduced and 14 have become law as of June 30, 2024.[15]

Some colleges have renamed their DEI departments, such as the Division of Access and Engagement at the University of Tennessee and the Office of Equal Opportunity Compliance and Engagement at Florida State University. However, administrators do not always draw a straight line between anti-DEI laws and the new names.[16] For some colleges, the changes may result from rethinking the goals of their programming given the needs of their communities after the pandemic. At other colleges, the impetus may have been a desire to avoid polarizing language while still reflecting the values of the institution.[17]

But Peter Lake, director of the Center for Excellence in Higher Education Law and Policy at Stetson University in Florida, cautioned in an *Inside Higher Ed* interview that the new labels for this work could soon become politicized as well.[18]

Scaling back on diversity initiatives may also create challenges for schools, colleges, and businesses where admission, hiring, and retention are concerned. As the population becomes increasingly diverse, more students and employees, particularly those from historically underrepresented groups, are seeking evidence that companies truly understand their needs. DEI programs can help provide that assurance.[19]

For independent schools, which often have more autonomy than government-funded institutions, this moment presents an opportunity to proactively articulate the vision, goals, and academic and community value of their work and to increase engagement across the school community.

QUESTIONS TO ASK

- What do diversity, equity, and inclusion mean at your school? What are your school's goals in the area of DEI? What work is needed at the leadership and governance levels to support your goals?
- DEI work often evolves to address changes in school life and culture. Have the goals and focus of your DEI work changed, and if so, how? What issues, topics, and opportunities are you engaging in now, and how have those changes impacted your legacy programs?
- How do you communicate about your DEI work? What do different constituent groups hear when you talk about it? What is your school's role in educating about civics and the 2024 election, and how does your DEI work contribute?
- What are some of the historical underpinnings of the contentious issues in today's civic debates? What is your school's role in educating about those histories, many of which helped shape today's DEI work?
- How does your school encourage open dialogue in classrooms and non-classroom settings? DEI work has long employed norms, principles, and other conversational guidelines to encourage civil discourse. What guidelines and training do you offer to faculty to help them foster civil discourse and teach about complex issues? How does your DEI programming support faculty (and student) development in this area?

STEPS TO TAKE

- Define and articulate the purpose of your school's DEI work. Communicate to all stakeholders the reasons for any changes as well as the issues or opportunities these changes seek to address.
- Evaluate how DEI is resourced in your school. If your school lacks the people and budget to achieve your goals, what actions can you take to secure the resources needed to meet your institutional goals?
- Dedicate time during full faculty and staff meetings to role-play and practice having conversations about contentious issues. Give teachers and administrators the training and support they need to mediate conflict and support complex conversations, including about antisemitism, Islamophobia, and other issues related to the war in Gaza.
- Determine whether your school needs civil discourse, cross-racial, and/or intercultural communication training to enhance the climate of inclusion on your campus.

MORE TO EXPLORE

Access further information here.

"2023-2024 State of Independent School Diversity Practice," Phillip Brooks, NAIS:
https://tinyurl.com/w7rbt9h7

2023-2024 State of Independent School Governance, Part 1: Board Composition, Membership, Policies, and Practices, **Margaret Anne Rowe and Amada Torres, NAIS:**
https://tinyurl.com/y3sw58ym

"How Polarization Affects Independent School Communities, Part 1: Polarization Through a Jobs-to-Be-Done Lens," Margaret Anne Rowe, NAIS:
https://www.nais.org/articles/pages/member/research/nais-research-how-polarization-affects-independent-school-communities-part-1/

Thriving in a World of Pluralistic Contention: A Framework for Schools, **John Austin et al., Edward E. Ford Foundation:**
https://www.eeford.org/a-framework-for-schools

ENDNOTES

[1] Phillip Brooks, "2023-2024 State of Independent School Diversity Practice," NAIS, January 2024; online at https://tinyurl.com/w7rbt9h7.

[2] Ibid.

[3] Ibid.

[4] Ibid.

[5] Ibid.

[6] Margaret Anne Rowe and Amada Torres, *2023-2024 State of Independent School Governance, Part 1: Board Composition, Membership, Policies, and Practices* (Washington, DC: NAIS, 2024); online at https://tinyurl.com/y3sw58ym.

[7] Brooks, "State of Independent School Diversity Practice."

[8] Stephen Sawchuk, "What Is Critical Race Theory, and Why Is It Under Attack?" *Education Week*, May 18, 2021; online at https://www.edweek.org/leadership/what-is-critical-race-theory-and-why-is-it-under-attack/2021/05.

[9] Margaret Anne Rowe and Joseph Corbett, "Hot Issues Survey: Challenges and Opportunities for Independent Schools," NAIS, Summer 2023; online at https://tinyurl.com/4crarjpz.

[10] Carroll Doherty et al., "Americans' Dismal Views of the Nation's Politics: Americans' Feelings About Politics, Polarization and the Tone of Political Discourse," Pew Research Center, September 19, 2023; online at https://www.pewresearch.org/politics/2023/09/19/americans-feelings-about-politics-polarization-and-the-tone-of-political-discourse/.

[11] Zacc Ritter, "Polarization May Undermine Community Bonds, Trust in Others," Gallup, February 19, 2020; online at https://news.gallup.com/opinion/gallup/284357/polarization-may-undermine-community-bonds-trust-others.aspx.

[12] Rowe and Corbett, "Hot Issues Survey."

[13] John Austin et al., *Thriving in a World of Pluralistic Contention: A Framework for Schools* (Brooklyn, NY: Edward E. Ford Foundation, 2024); online at https://www.eeford.org/a-framework-for-schools.

[14] Sarah Kessler, "D.E.I. Goes Quiet," *The New York Times*, January 15, 2024; online at https://www.nytimes.com/2024/01/13/business/dealbook/dei-goes-quiet.html.

[15] *The Chronicle of Higher Education*, "DEI Legislation Tracker," accessed July 18, 2024; online at https://www.chronicle.com/article/here-are-the-states-where-lawmakers-are-seeking-to-ban-colleges-dei-efforts.

[16] Stephanie Saul, "With State Bans on D.E.I., Some Universities Find a Workaround: Rebranding," *The New York Times*, April 12, 2024; online at https://www.nytimes.com/2024/04/12/us/diversity-ban-dei-college.html.

[17] Johanna Alonso, "Are DEI Office Name Changes Enough?" *Inside Higher Ed*, April 10, 2024; online at https://www.insidehighered.com/news/government/state-policy/2024/04/10/diversity-office-name-changes-spark-concern-both-sides.

[18] Ibid.

[19] Kiara Alfonseca and Max Zahn, "How Corporate America Is Slashing DEI Workers Amid Backlash to Diversity Programs," *ABC News*, July 7, 2023; online at https://abcnews.go.com/US/corporate-america-slashing-dei-workers-amid-backlash-diversity/story?id=100477952.

6

The Artificial Intelligence Forecast

By Tim Fish and Jackie Wolking

Tim Fish served as NAIS's chief innovation officer until July 2024.

Jackie Wolking is director of innovation programs.

Key Takeaways

- Schools cannot say no to artificial intelligence. AI is inevitable. Independent schools will need to provide training on how to use it, incorporate its use into policies and procedures, and figure out where it aligns with the educational mission.
- As schools use AI to handle some creative and administrative tasks, they will make changes both to what tasks they do and who does them. The result is likely to be a reorganization of human capital, including investing in some areas and possibly reimagining others.
- Teaching is an area in which AI offers great promise but also great challenges. Building an AI-rich environment will lead to reimagining the role of the teacher. The key is to make the highest use of teachers' abilities, including guiding, offering feedback, and building relationships that make learning collaborative and relevant.

Schools Need to Develop Their Vision for AI and Its Many Ramifications

The world changed on November 30, 2022, when OpenAI released ChatGPT. According to Reuters, the new app took only two months to reach the 100-million active user mark, a new record. To put that number in perspective, it took TikTok nine months to reach the same milestone and Instagram 2.5 years.[1] Many of us will never forget the first time we typed a question into the prompt box and watched the GPT magically weave together a response. In modern tech history, it can only be compared to the first time we used an internet browser and watched a web page download.

In a 2024 blog post, strategic technology consultant Eric Hudson reflected on MIT's classification of generative AI "as an 'arrival' technology (like smartphones or the internet) and not as an 'adoption' technology (like smart boards or learning management systems)." He went on to say,

> We should recognize that we are not in a position to decide if AI should be in our schools or not. Like the arrival technologies that preceded it, AI is and will become deeply integrated into our lives, often in ways we are barely aware of. Students (and everyone else who works in a school) will use AI regardless of a school's position or policies.[2]

The inevitability of AI leads to many questions—questions being discussed not only by independent schools but also by educational institutions around the world. How do schools move forward in a world where generative AI will always be immediately available to every student—in their pocket or on their wrist? How will AI impact everything from operations to classroom teaching? What should the school day look like, and how will teachers assess students' work? How do schools need to change so that students develop AI-related skills in addition to human capabilities like empathy, integrity, resilience, and reliability?

Schools will be grappling with such questions for years to come. But one thing is certain: They cannot say no to AI. Rather, schools need to determine how AI can enhance rather than inhibit their educational mission. This means that each school will have to determine the correct alignment of emerging tech with its values, explain how tech is a tool to help the school become a better version of itself, and make it clear to the community that the school continues to support the development of the whole child.

It also means that schools have to provide training for faculty and staff. They must take steps to protect student privacy and limit unintentional harm. And school leaders and boards must knowledgeably and nimbly develop policies, procedures, and beliefs to navigate transparency, trust, bias, and ethics in rapidly developing technologies.

To accomplish all this, educators need a deep understanding of what AI can do and where it needs to be managed. Leaders need to shape policies from a place of understanding rather than fear. AI is not good at everything; it can be comical to watch it fail in some areas.[3] There are places where AI can unleash human potential and other places where it can undermine community and jeopardize safety. Each school needs to find the appropriate balance for its community.

AI Is Likely to Change How the School Does Its Non-Classroom Work

AI is changing, and will continue to change, what professionals do in settings that range from hospitals to law offices to engineering firms. As the *Wall Street Journal* put it:

> Large language models like OpenAI's ChatGPT, Google's Gemini and a host of industry- or task-specific software are slowly being embedded into more Americans' daily tasks. In some cases the tools are helping people do their jobs better and faster. In others they are making people do their jobs differently.[4]

For many people, AI is quickly becoming a work partner—crafting first drafts, analyzing data, and creating meeting summaries. Professionals are finding ways to use AI to do the tedious work they dread, freeing up more time to focus on tasks that maximize their value and experience.

Schools are no exception. Even as they grapple with fundamental questions about this new technology, some schools are putting AI to work in practical ways to increase efficiency.

The proliferation of specialized AI assistants is helping schools with a variety of creative and administrative tasks. For example, AI tools can help with marketing and communication efforts, creating stunning visuals or writing different versions of messages for different audiences. Chatbots can connect prospective families to ways to schedule visits or to learn about specific resources that match their interests. AI can create automated email newsletters that keep parents of enrolled students informed of school activities. HR managers can more quickly search for candidates and vet applications.

Leveraging AI for task completion has the potential to disrupt the labor market, however. In the business world, companies are primarily relying on off-the-shelf solutions, such as ChatGPT, to gain efficiencies and improve existing activities.[5] Schools' use of AI could alter the hiring model as individuals' capacities shift and tech takes on more and more tasks. In an article in the *Stanford Social Innovation Review*, the authors speculate that "jobs with routine elements, such as in regulatory compliance or clerical work, and those that involve simple data collection, data summary, and writing tasks are likely to disappear."[6]

As AI Becomes More of an Embedded Student-Tutor, Schools Need to Reconsider How They Design Learning Experiences

The existence of AI challenges a fundamental paradigm in K-12 education: Traditionally, school is the place students go to acquire knowledge from a teacher. But the new reality of AI raises still more inevitable questions related to teaching and learning. What if AI can create a learning environment where students can learn on their own, at their own pace, with a personal tutor who has infinite patience and a deep understanding of how they learn best? What new skills will students need to develop to effectively learn from an AI tool?

And what will independent schools and teachers need to do to be an essential part of learning and teaching?

For one thing, there are important skills that teachers can provide in an AI-enabled future. Respondents to a 2023 survey conducted by Microsoft identified the top skills likely to be most important in an AI-embedded future:

- Analytical judgment
- Flexibility
- Emotional intelligence
- Critical evaluation
- Intellectual curiosity
- Bias detection and handling
- AI delegation[7]

Teachers need to instill these skills in order to become facilitators of each student's personal journey with AI. In this view of the future, the focus of great teachers will be on the relationships they build and how they help students see the real-world applications of knowledge. Students will first receive content in bite-sized formats tailored to what they need in the moment. AI tutors won't give students answers, but they will provide suggestions and prompts to unlock critical thinking. They might ask students to explain problems in multiple ways, help them organize their thinking through various frameworks, or even gamify a situation to make the content more engaging.

As students initially learn concepts, it will be the role of the teacher to monitor progress, provide thought-provoking feedback, engage students in discussion, and make learning collaborative and relevant. To ensure that students don't become overreliant on the technology in this AI-enriched environment, teachers will need to continuously push activities that promote cognitive rigor, interdependent work with peers, and meta-learning (learning how to learn).

What will all this look like? The Center for Curriculum Redesign (CCR) recently revised its 4D competencies framework that highlights what teachers should emphasize in an AI world. CCR advocates that teachers focus on adaptability, making the point that

> human adaptability involves the capacity to deal with a number of different sources of data and modes of reasoning that AI cannot muster yet. Human decision-making is also deeply intertwined with emotions and social understandings, areas where AI currently lacks proficiency.[8]

So shifts in the educator experience will be inevitable. Educators will have to upskill around AI literacy to ensure that they are teaching students how to best leverage these emerging technologies. Similarly, teachers will have to effectively navigate these systems in a number of ways.

For example, imagine a scenario in which AI functions as a teaching assistant or co-teacher providing targeted instruction and support based on each child's unique needs. This is what is currently happening in schools across the country that are delivering literacy instruction via voice-enabled AI bots.[9] Also consider the vast amounts of data collected on student learning with AI (e.g., questions asked, content mastered, misunderstandings corrected, etc.) and how that new information is reported and ultimately used to support a student.

These scenarios require teachers to have a certain level of openness to and comfort with technology in the classroom. Teachers will also need resourcefulness and strategic decision-making ability so they can monitor highly individualized and divergent learning paths.

IN JIM COLLINS' GROUNDBREAKING BOOK *Good to Great*, he explains that technology can serve as an accelerator—but not as a creator—of greatness.[10] In other words, the right technology can enhance and speed up progress, but it cannot turn a mediocre organization into a great one on its own.

The same is true for AI. It can help a school live its mission more fully, but it cannot create a great school on its own. As schools move forward in an AI-embedded world, leaders must thoughtfully debate how new technologies fit with a reimagined learning experience in an increasingly AI-driven future. It's an exciting time, full of potential for transformation. The challenge lies in navigating this landscape with wisdom, creativity, and a steadfast commitment to the mission of the school and the holistic development of each student.

QUESTIONS TO ASK

- What's your response when board members or parents ask how AI will impact your school or how you plan to use it?
- What skills will be even more important for students to develop as AI use increases?
- How should the use of AI tools differ in different grade levels—lower, middle, and high school?
- As you integrate AI into your school over the next few years, how will roles and positions evolve? How can AI enable teachers to deepen their relationships with students and increase personalized learning?
- What AI pitfalls are most likely to impact the way you use it in your school?
- Within your school's market, how might AI create

disruptive new entrants that compete with your school for students or employees?

- What does change management look like at your school?

STEPS TO TAKE

- Try using AI every day to get accustomed to its potential. For example, research a topic. Draft an email. Come up with five good questions about pressing topics. Query AI to have it act as a board member who asks you tough questions. Or find the personality that works for you: Ask AI to respond to your questions as your favorite actor, philosopher, writer, etc., and see how the responses change.
- Investigate options in different AI categories to better understand them. These could include writing, reading, and math instruction; assessment and grading; data and infrastructure; curiosity and engagement; the school-home connection; and teacher productivity tools and professional development.
- Convene an AI task force to discuss the alignment between AI/tech and your school's mission and values. Include varied stakeholders from varied perspectives. Create a safe space where complexity and ambiguity can be explored.
- Consider these recommendations from Deloitte to mitigate the risks of implementing AI:
    - Monitor regulatory requirements and ensure compliance, particularly around data security and student privacy.
    - Establish a framework for the use of generative AI tools and applications.
    - Conduct internal audits and testing on generative AI tools and applications.
    - Train practitioners in how to recognize and mitigate potential risks.
    - Ensure that a human validates all generative AI content.[11]

MORE TO EXPLORE

Access further information here.

"AI Initiative: Understanding the Impact of AI on Our Kids," Common Sense Media:
https://www.commonsensemedia.org/ai

"Bringing AI to Schools: Tips for School Leaders," ISTE (International Society for Technology in Education):
https://tinyurl.com/yudb2z93

***Co-Intelligence: Living & Working with AI,* Ethan Mollick**

***Education for the Age of AI,* Charles Fadel et al., Center for Curriculum Redesign**

"Your AI Resource Hub," ATLIS (Association of Technology Leaders in Independent Schools):
https://theatlis.org/page/ai

ENDNOTES

[1] Krystal Hu, "ChatGPT Sets Record for Fastest-Growing User Base—Analyst Note," Reuters, February 2, 2023; online at https://www.reuters.com/technology/chatgpt-sets-record-fastest-growing-user-base-analyst-note-2023-02-01/.

[2] Eric Hudson, "Looking Ahead with AI, Part 2: Students," *Learning on Purpose* blog, May 10, 2024; online at https://erichudson.substack.com/p/looking-ahead-with-ai-part-2-students.

[3] A lawyer who submitted a brief written by ChatGPT probably did not find it comical when it was discovered that the brief contained several "hallucitations"—precedents that looked like legitimate law cases but did not actually exist. The lawyer paid a steep fine. Benjamin Weiser, "Here's What Happens When Your Lawyer Uses ChatGPT," *The New York Times*, May 27, 2023; online at https://www.nytimes.com/2023/05/27/nyregion/avianca-airline-lawsuit-chatgpt.html.

[4] Ray A. Smith and Lauren Weber, "How AI Has Already Begun to Change These Workers' Jobs," *The Wall Street Journal*, May 8, 2024.

[5] Deborshi Dott et al., *The State of Generative AI in the Enterprise: Now Decides Next* (New York: Deloitte, 2024); online at https://www2.deloitte.com/content/dam/Deloitte/us/Documents/consulting/us-state-of-gen-ai-report.pdf.

[6] Daron Acemoglu and Simon Johnson, "Choosing AI's Impact on the Future of Work," *Stanford Social Innovation Review*, October 25, 2023; online at https://ssir.org/articles/entry/ai-impact-on-jobs-and-work.

[7] Goh Chiew Tong, "Here Are the Top Skills You Will Need for an 'A.I.-Powered Future,' According to New Microsoft Data," CNBC, May 9, 2023; online at https://www.cnbc.com/2023/05/09/top-skills-you-will-need-for-an-ai-powered-future-according-to-microsoft-.html.

[8] The core principle of CCR's 4D competencies framework is that students must develop in four dimensions—knowledge, skills, character, and meta-learning—to best serve themselves and society. Center for Curriculum Redesign, "4D Competencies Framework," January 2024;

ON THE HORIZON

AI will continue to evolve with mind-boggling speed. Between 2021 and 2024, investors poured $330 billion into about 26,000 AI and machine-learning startups.[12] Game-changing technology is sure to follow. For example, OpenAI is developing ChatGPT Edu, a version of its AI platform for higher ed.[13] It's easy to imagine that a version for K-12 schools could follow soon.

Schools will need ways to teach in the age of deepfakes. One method is called "prebunking," a term invented by University of Cambridge psychologist Sander van der Linden in his book *Foolproof: Why Misinformation Infects Our Minds and How to Build Immunity*. Exposure to and practice with misinformation can inoculate students against future falsified information.[14] Another tactic gaining popularity is watermarking, which aims to flag deepfakes on the internet.[15]

Students will need help navigating the incredible amount of information at their fingertips. In his *Learning on Purpose* blog, Eric Hudson writes, "Looking ahead to how we want to engage students on AI in the coming year, we should focus less on controlling their use of AI and more on nurturing their autonomy."[16] He recommends educator Rosetta Eun Ryong Lee's "A Young Person's Guide to Autonomy," which offers suggestions for when to rely on oneself, when to go to peers, and when to ask an adult.[17]

online at https://curriculumredesign.org/frameworks/competencies-framework/.

[9] Olina Banerji, "Schools Are Using Voice Technology to Teach Reading. Is It Helping?" *EdSurge*, March 7, 2023; online at https://www.edsurge.com/news/2023-03-07-schools-are-using-voice-technology-to-teach-reading-is-it-helping.

[10] Jim Collins, *Good to Great: Why Some Companies Make the Leap... and Others Don't* (New York: HarperCollins, 2001).

[11] Dott et al., *State of Generative AI.*

[12] Cade Metz, Karen Weise, and Tripp Mickle, "A.I. Start-Ups Face a Rough Financial Reality Check," *The New York Times*, April 29, 2024; online at https://www.nytimes.com/2024/04/29/technology/ai-startups-financial-reality.html.

[13] Open AI, "Introducing ChatGPT Edu," May 30, 2024; online at https://openai.com/index/introducing-chatgpt-edu/.

[14] Sander van der Linden, *Foolproof: Why Misinformation Infects Our Minds and How to Build Immunity* (New York, W.W. Norton & Co., 2023). Cited in Greg Rosalsky, "How Do You Counter Misinformation? Critical Thinking Is Step One," National Public Radio, April 30, 2024; online at https://www.npr.org/sections/money/2024/04/30/1247565565/how-do-you-counter-misinformation-critical-thinking-is-step-one.

[15] Rosalsky, "How Do You Counter Misinformation?"

[16] Hudson, "Looking Ahead with AI."

[17] Rosetta Eun Ryong Lee, "A Young Person's Guide to Autonomy," May 3, 2024; online at https://tinyurl.com/4bw85saj.

7

The Higher Education Forecast

By Debra P. Wilson

Debra P. Wilson is president of NAIS.

Key Takeaways

- The standardized testing landscape has been in flux since the pandemic. As colleges have shifted from test mandatory to test free to everything in between, applicants (and college counselors) have struggled to find the best approach. And testing companies are laying the groundwork for big changes in how and what to assess.
- The growth in applications and other changes make it harder to predict where students will be admitted, which increases stress for families. It also makes it even more important to manage expectations and articulate the value of independent schools beyond college admission.
- As tuition rises, some families and students have grown skeptical about the value of higher education, particularly at costly private colleges. This skepticism manifests itself in alternative ways to prepare for careers through new means of education and training.

Disruption in the Education Landscape Is Reigniting Debates Around Standardized Assessment

Trends in higher education admission can inform how independent schools design programming, think about the student experience, and talk about the purpose of independent schools. This chapter looks at three influential trends in higher education that could affect even elementary grades.

The pandemic set off an earthquake in the realm of higher education standardized tests when it suddenly and significantly hastened the burgeoning test-optional movement. After safety and logistical concerns prevented many students from taking the tests in person for the 2020-2021 application cycle, two-thirds of colleges and universities chose to go test optional, test blind, or test free.

When most colleges decided to go, and then stay, test optional, they reignited the longstanding debate around the value of tests like the SAT and ACT—specifically whether these tests favor white and wealthy students. But in the early months of 2024, the debate began to shift. New research convinced some university leaders that while not perfect, these tests provide a way to demonstrate readiness for college that is actually *less* influenced by privilege than other parts of the application, such as essays and teacher recommendations. Ivy League schools have been the main driver of the shift as they have looked for ways to both diversify their classes and assess academic capability amid a tidal wave of applications[1] (see next section). So while at least 1,825 four-year colleges in the U.S.—more than 80%—will not require SAT or ACT scores for fall 2025, a handful of highly selective colleges have reinstated the requirement.[2]

For students and families, these fast-moving changes have been confusing and not always well communicated. Figuring out how college admission officers view the changes is hard, particularly for applicants to test-optional institutions. Students who would expect to do well on standardized tests can no longer count on the value of their high scores in the process, and those who choose not to submit scores are unsure about how admission officers will view a lack of test outcomes. This has added one more element of ambiguity to an already-stressful process for families.

For schools, the changes mean a shift in how they support students in the college admission process. The debate about assessment has also compelled many schools to rethink how they talk about student outcomes and independent schools' own value propositions.

For the organizations that offer assessment tests, the sudden drop-off in testing has presented both a financial and an existential threat. That threat has prompted some of them to make substantial shifts in the format and administration of their tests and to rethink—or accelerate—their plans for change.

- The nonprofit ACT was recently acquired by a private equity group and now intends to focus on providing resources in the area of career readiness and other kinds of skills assessment.[3] In addition, in July 2024 ACT announced it would shorten the test by 44 questions and make the science portion optional.[4]
- The College Board, the organization behind the SAT and the AP, recently shortened the SAT test and is transitioning it to an all-digital format.[5]
- The Educational Testing Service (ETS), which works closely with the College Board as well as the government to create, administer, and measure standardized tests, has recently announced plans to expand its resources in career readiness and assessment, as well as in certification. ETS also intends to broaden its approach to assessment in the K-12 space.[6]

This disruption to the business of assessment comes as many entities, including independent schools, are recognizing the value of measuring skills, traits, and knowledge in new ways, as well as focusing more intently on preparing students for the careers of tomorrow. (See "On the Horizon" at the end of this chapter for more on this.)

Shifts in College Application Trends Create Ambiguity for K-12 Schools and Students

In addition to changes in colleges' testing requirements, a number of other trends surrounding admission are causing more ambiguity, less predictable outcomes, and new sources of stress for students and families.

Applications—and competition—are surging. Likely due in part to the removal of the testing requirement at many colleges, overall applications have jumped in recent years. In 2023-2024 alone, the number of applications submitted to institutions that use the Common App grew by 6%

compared to the previous year. Applications were up 10% at public universities and 5% at private institutions.[7] Compared to 2019-2020—the last year unaffected by the pandemic—there has been an overall 28% increase in applications submitted through the Common App.[8]

Colleges are seeing continued growth in early action (EA) and early decision (ED) applications.* In 2023-2024 the number of EA and ED applications submitted via the Common App was nearly equal to those submitted for regular decision. Applications for the first round of EA and ED had increased by 38% compared to 2019, and second-round applications had increased by 90%.[9]

Defying expectations, applications from underrepresented minorities have increased. One anticipated trend appears not to have materialized. Concerns grew about less diversity among applicants following two June 2023 Supreme Court decisions that ended race-conscious admission in colleges: *Students for Fair Admissions, Inc. (SFFA) v. President & Fellows of Harvard College (Harvard)* and *SFFA v. University of North Carolina.* In fact, 2023-2024 saw 10% more applicants from underrepresented minority groups than the year before. First-generation applicants increased by 4%.[10]

Legacy and other forms of admission favoritism continue to be controversial. In 2023, the nonprofit Opportunity Insights released a study about the effects of financial, legacy, or athlete status—as well as private school attendance—on admission to highly selective colleges. The study concluded that applicants with any one or more of these characteristics were considerably more likely to be accepted to a highly selective college, even when standardized test scores and grades were similar.[11] This research led to questions about whether these colleges could have accepted more highly qualified students of color or students with more socioeconomic diversity but chose not to.[12] Some colleges and universities have since decided to discontinue legacy admission, and some state legislatures have mandated that they do so.[13]

How are these trends playing out in independent schools? A fall 2023 NAIS survey of independent school college counselors found the following:

---

* *Early action* and *early decision* both offer students an early response, but they differ in the level of commitment required. Early action is nonbinding, allowing a student to apply early and receive a decision without committing to enroll. Early decision is binding—if accepted at the college or university, the student must attend.

FIGURE 1

Changes in the College Admission Process Since the Pandemic

WHAT INDEPENDENT SCHOOL COUNSELORS REPORT SEEING SINCE 2019-2020

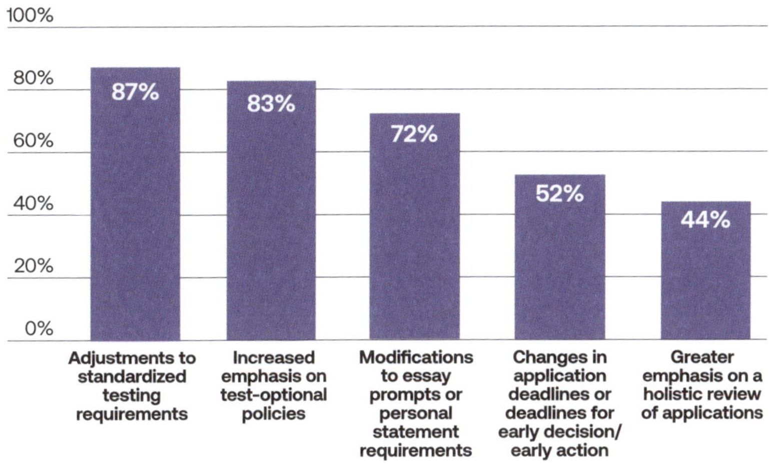

Source: Joe Corbett, "Trends in College Admission," NAIS

- Eighty-seven percent of respondents reported changes to testing requirements at the colleges students were applying to.
- Eighty-three percent noted an increased emphasis on test-optional policies.
- More than half (52%) reported changes in the deadlines for early action and early decision, and many said the deadlines were earlier, increasing the pressure on students to make an important college decision earlier in the process.[14]

With the admissions pool at highly selective colleges so large, the acceptance rates have dropped accordingly. In addition, the test-optional policies have driven average test scores up as those students who expect to do well are more likely to submit their scores, thus increasing the pressure on students. In the absence of universal requirements for test scores, many students are choosing to do *more*—taking on *more* extracurricular activities and submitting *more* applications to *more* competitive schools. One college counselor commented that students feel that "every little move during high

FIGURE 2

Changes in Students' College Decisions Since the Pandemic

INDEPENDENT SCHOOL COUNSELORS REPORTING INCREASES SINCE 2019-2020

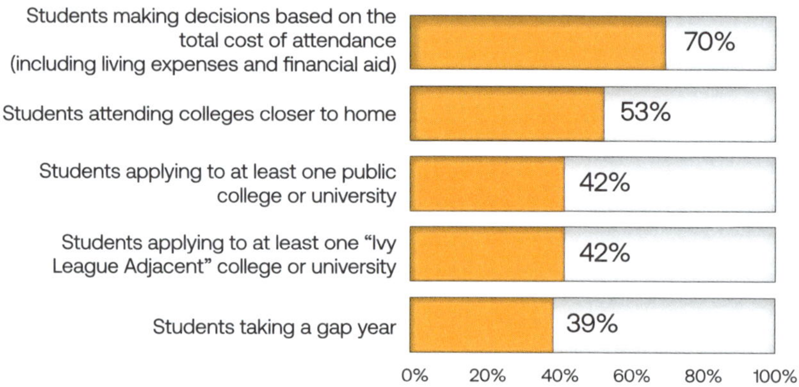

Source: Joe Corbett, "Trends in College Admission," NAIS

school ... might impact college admission." All of this increases the ambiguity of the application process and the anxiety of students and their families.[15]

The Public Continues to Question the Cost and Benefits of Higher Education

As the price tag for college has gone up, student loan debt has accumulated, and options for work-based training have expanded, Americans appear to be increasingly skeptical about the value of traditional higher education. For the first time in its history, the University of Chicago's nonpartisan NORC survey found that the majority (56%) of Americans do not believe that college is worth the cost. Respondents indicated that they believe people often graduate with nonspecific skills and a large amount of debt.[16] But doubts about higher education are not universal. In a 2023 report from Gallup and the Walton Family Foundation, 83% of Generation Z (born between 1997 and 2012) said that a college education today is "very important" or "fairly important."[17] This may signal that attendance patterns are not changing any time soon among the majority of the very generation looking to go to college in the near future.

Nevertheless, two issues are causing the public to think hard about what a college diploma gets them, especially at select private colleges with considerably higher overall costs.

Affordability. In the 2023-2024 school year, when all expenses were considered, the total cost to attend a handful of private colleges approached $100,000.[18] Admittedly, these are the very highest of price tags, and those colleges are quick to point out the amount of financial aid they give. But between 1980 and 2020, the average price of tuition, fees, and room and board for an undergraduate degree increased by 169%, according to the Georgetown University Center on Education and the Workforce.[19] These soaring prices are likely to hit particularly hard for parents who are millennials (born between 1981 and 1996), as their generation bears much of the $1.75 trillion in total student loan debt in the U.S.[20]

As a private college experience has become increasingly costly, one outcome has been an increase in the popularity of flagship state universities, including among out-of-state applicants.[21] For in-state students, the growth of honors colleges and state-specific scholarships has given exceptional students more incentives to stay near home.[22]

In the NAIS research referenced above, college counselors' responses seem to affirm that some of these trends are reflected in independent schools. For example, when asked about changes since the start of school year 2019-2020, 70% of respondents said the number of students making college decisions based on the total cost of attendance had increased, and 53% noted that more students were attending colleges closer to home.[23] These decisions may be impacting parents' perceptions of the competitiveness of colleges to which independent school students are admitted and attend (Figure 2).

Career-readiness. Once college students invest in tuition and have their diplomas in hand, will employers think they're prepared—and qualified—for the world of work? Questions like this have led to an expansion of options for work-based education, credentials, and training. Some companies offer to help finance a degree at a two- or four-year college or to provide on-the-job training for hard-to-fill jobs.

While work-based training has been available for decades, what's new and notable are the white-collar apprenticeships emerging in fields traditionally popular with four-year college graduates, such as finance, cybersecurity, and consulting. *The Wall Street Journal* described such programs under the headline "More Students Are Turning Away from College and Toward Apprenticeships: Some White-Collar Training Programs Have Become as Selective as Ivy League Universities." Among the selective programs cited, one insurance firm hired 92 apprentices out of 800 applications; another apprenticeship program drew 1,500 applicants for 100 positions—a 7% acceptance rate.[24]

For school leaders seeking to best support their students, it's important to continue to track the changing perceptions about higher education as well as the trends in which colleges students ultimately attend. Doing so will help the school speak effectively to families not only about the decisions families and students make about college but also, and perhaps more importantly, about the school's mission and goals for its students beyond—or even instead of—college acceptance. Some schools have been effective in changing the narrative to focus on the skills and habits of mind that will help students thrive in the next step in their educational and life journey.

What happens in higher education admission has a very real effect on independent schools in two ways: It shapes how parents and students perceive the value of their independent school experiences. And it also influences how schools prepare students for the next chapter in their education, whether that is attending an Ivy League university or a state college or participating in work-based or on-the-job training. Inevitably, many families will continue to be focused on having their children go on to highly selective colleges and universities. However, it is up to each school to support whatever choice will offer each student the best opportunity for long-term and lifetime success.

QUESTIONS TO ASK

- How do you demonstrate your school's value to families, particularly as it relates to preparing students to succeed in college and beyond? In general, how do higher education trends impact how you communicate your mission and core values?
- What are families' expectations regarding standardized tests? How do you communicate about these topics?
- How is your school educating families about the shifts taking place in higher education so that you can manage their expectations of the admission process,

expenses, and potential outcomes? What subtle cues are you giving students about the quality of their choices of next steps?

- What programmatic changes are you making to ensure that your students also develop the habits of mind and other skills, traits, and characteristics beyond traditional assessment, with the ultimate goal of helping them thrive as adults?

STEPS TO TAKE

- Continue to maintain relationships with a wide range of colleges and universities.
- Set expectations early with parents and students around college admission.
- Broaden your communications about the scope of schools and options your students may consider after high school. Ensure that other signals, such as posters, communications, and celebrations, reinforce this array of choices.
- Consider the skills, traits, and knowledge your students will need to be successful in the future, and design programming that will equip them for whatever path they choose after high school.

MORE TO EXPLORE

Access further information here.

"Affirmative Action for the 1%," Michael Barbaro, *The New York Times*:
https://www.nytimes.com/2023/07/27/podcasts/the-daily/college-legacy-admissions.html

Association of College Counselors in Independent Schools:
https://www.accisnet.org

***Charting the Future of Assessments*, Patrick C. Kyllonen and Amit Sevak, ETS Research Institute:**
https://www.ets.org/Rebrand/pdf/FoA_Full_Report.pdf

"Developing Trend: How Will Changes in Higher Education

ON THE HORIZON

Partnerships are accelerating innovation in assessment, which may change the way both K-12 schools and colleges evaluate students. In 2023-2024, the Carnegie Foundation for the Advancement of Teaching announced a partnership with the Educational Testing Service (ETS) to focus on building new tools to assess disciplinary knowledge and skills that are predictors of workforce success. The partnership also intends to focus on developing a skills-based transcript.[25]

In addition, ETS has acquired the Mastery Transcript Consortium (MTC), the entity founded by Scott Looney, head of Hawken School (OH), and used by many independent schools. MTC offers an alternative K-12 transcript based on student mastery and portfolios of specific skills, competencies, and knowledge.[26]

Colleges will continue to experiment with other approaches to admissions. Direct admissions—through which colleges and universities review student profiles or portfolios and offer students a place *before* they apply—continue to gain ground and may help attract more diverse classes and cut out most of the traditional processes. Students must meet certain academic and, sometimes, demographic requirements.[27]

Affect Your Independent School?" NAIS:
https://www.nais.org/articles/pages/member/how-will-changes-in-higher-education-affect-your-independent-school/

"Diversifying Society's Leaders? The Determinants and Causal Effects of Admission to Highly Selective Private Colleges," Raj Chetty et al., Opportunity Insights:
https://opportunityinsights.org/wp-content/uploads/2023/07/CollegeAdmissions_Paper.pdf

"Is College Worth It?" Richard Fry et al., Pew Research Center:
https://www.pewresearch.org/social-trends/2024/05/23/is-college-worth-it-2/#:~:text=At%20a%20time%20when%20many,over%20the%20past%2010%20years

ENDNOTES

[1] Sarah Wood, "Some Colleges Are Requiring Test Scores Again: What It Means for Applicants," *U.S. News & World Report*, May 13, 2024; online at https://www.usnews.com/education/best-colleges/applying/articles/some-colleges-are-requiring-test-scores-again-what-it-means-for-applicants.

[2] FairTest, "Test Optional and Test Free College List"; online at https://fairtest.org/test-optional-list/.

[3] Liam Knox, "What's Behind the ACT's For-Profit Pivot?" *Inside Higher Ed*, April 25, 2024; online at https://www.insidehighered.com/news/admissions/traditional-age/2024/04/25/acts-private-equity-takeover-and-future-testing.

[4] Janet Godwin, "The ACT Test Is Evolving," ACT Newsroom & Blog, July 15, 2024; online at https://leadershipblog.act.org/2024/07/test-enhancements.html.

[5] Elissa Nadworny, "Starting in 2024, U.S. Students Will Take the SAT Entirely Online," NPR, January 25, 2022; online at https://www.npr.org/2022/01/25/1075315337/new-digital-sat-college-admissions-test-requirement-2024-us.

[6] Patrick C. Kyllonen and Amit Sevak, *Charting the Future of Assessments* (Princeton, NJ: ETS Research Institute, 2024); online at https://www.ets.org/Rebrand/pdf/FoA_Full_Report.pdf.

[7] Brian Heseung Kim et al., "Deadline Updates, 2023-2024: First-Year Application Trends Through March 1," Common App, March 14, 2024; online at https://www.commonapp.org/files/Common-App-Deadline-Updates-2024.03.01.pdf.

[8] Michael T. Nietzel, "College Applications Are Up Significantly for Next Fall," *Forbes*, April 1, 2024; online at https://www.forbes.com/sites/michaeltnietzel/2024/04/01/college-applications-are-up-significantly-for-next-fall/.

[9] Liam Knox, "Early Application Data Are Rosy, If Complex," *Inside Higher Ed*, November 16, 2023; online at https://www.insidehighered.com/news/admissions/traditional-age/2023/11/16/early-admissions-data-show-big-bump-applications#.

[10] Nietzel, "College Applications Are Up Significantly."

[11] Raj Chetty, David J. Deming, and John N. Friedman, "Diversifying Society's Leaders? The Determinants and Causal Effects of Admission to Highly Selective Private Colleges," Opportunity Insights, October 2023; online at https://opportunityinsights.org/wp-content/uploads/2023/07/CollegeAdmissions_Paper.pdf.

[12] Aatish Bhatia, Claire Cain Miller, and Josh Katz, "Study of Elite College Admissions Data Suggests Being Very Rich Is Its Own Qualification," *The New York Times*, July 24, 2023; online at https://www.nytimes.com/interactive/2023/07/24/upshot/ivy-league-elite-college-admissions.html.

[13] Hallie Miller and Olivia Sanchez, "Maryland Becomes the Third State to Completely Ban Legacy Preference in Admissions," *The Hechinger Report*, May 1, 2024; online at https://hechingerreport.org/maryland-to-become-the-third-state-to-completely-ban-legacy-preference-in-admissions/.

[14] Joe Corbett, "Trends in College Admission," NAIS, Winter 2024; online at https://www.nais.org/getmedia/854728e8-80e3-4e64-b3ad-45c9d59f685e/NAIS-Research_Trends-in-College-Admission_2-2024.pdf.

[15] Ibid.

[16] Douglas Belkin, "Americans Are Losing Faith in College Education, WSJ-NORC Poll Finds," *The Wall Street Journal*, March 31, 2023; online at https://www.wsj.com/articles/americans-are-losing-faith-in-college-education-wsj-norc-poll-finds-3a836ce1?st=mtsj6ht9e2dbe6u&reflink=desktopwebshare_permalink.

[17] Gallup and Walton Family Foundation, "Voices of Gen Z: Perspectives on U.S. Education, Wellbeing and the Future," 2023; online at https://www.gallup.com/file/analytics/510701/gallup-walton-family-foundation-voices-of-gen-z-report.aspx.

[18] Josh Moody, "Inching Toward the $100,000 Sticker Price," *Inside Higher Ed*, April 3, 2024; online at https://www.insidehighered.com/news/business/revenue-strategies/2024/04/03/inching-toward-100000-sticker-price.

[19] Nicole Goodkind, "Some Colleges Cost $95,000 per Year, and They're Only Getting More Expensive. Here's Why," CNN Business, July 16, 2023; online at https://www.cnn.com/2023/07/16/investing/curious-consumer-college-cost/index.html.

[20] Alicia Hahn, "2024 Student Loan Debt Statistics: Average Student Loan Debt," *Forbes Advisor*, April 18, 2024; online at https://www.forbes.com/advisor/student-loans/average-student-loan-debt-statistics/.

[21] Aaron Klein, "The Great Student Swap," *Brookings Mountain West*, September 2022; online at https://www.brookings.edu/wp-content/uploads/2022/08/Final-_GreatStudentSwap_9-6-22.pdf.

[22] Jenny Brundin, "How Do We Get Colorado Students to Pursue Higher Education and Work in State?" CPR News, March 12, 2024; online at https://www.cpr.org/2024/03/12/how-to-make-college-tuition-more-affordable-for-coloradans/.

[23] Corbett, "Trends in College Admission."

[24] Douglas Belkin, "More Students Are Turning Away from College and Toward Apprenticeships: Some White-Collar Training Programs Have Become as Selective as Ivy League Universities," *The Wall Street Journal*, March 16, 2024; online at https://www.wsj.com/articles/more-students-are-turning-away-from-college-and-toward-apprenticeships-15f3a05d?st=j9a4ys2l6l7fclu&reflink=article_email_share.

[25] Beth Hawkins, "74 Interview: Time ≠ Learning—Tim Knowles on Scrapping the Carnegie Unit," *The 74 Newsletter*, September 5, 2023; online at https://www.the74million.org/article/74-interview-time-≠-learning-tim-knowles-on-scrapping-the-carnegie-unit/.

[26] Tom Vander Ark, "Skills Transcripts at Scale: Why the ETS & MTC Partnership Is a Big Deal," *Getting Smart* blog, May 15, 2024; online at https://www.gettingsmart.com/2024/05/15/skills-transcripts-at-scale-why-the-ets-mtc-partnership-is-a-big-deal/.

[27] Sarah Wood, "College Direct Admissions: What to Know," *U.S. News & World Report*, December 12, 2023; online at https://tinyurl.com/yd3fvv43.

PART 2

This section offers snapshots of key data points that illuminate the state of independent schools.

Snapshot Authors

Phillip Brooks, research analyst at NAIS

Margaret Anne Rowe, senior research analyst

Grant Stringer, research analyst

Amada Torres, vice president for studies, insights, and research

Demographics

Independent schools are feeling the squeeze as the pool of school-age children shrinks and families leave large metro areas.

FERTILITY RATES ARE DOWN FOR WOMEN ACROSS ALL LEVELS OF INCOME AND EDUCATION

2.07
Average total fertility rate in **2008**

1.66
Average total fertility rate in **2022**

Sources: Federal Reserve Bank of St. Louis, "Fertility Rate, Total for the United States," and Michelle J.K. Osterman, "Births: Final Data for 2022," Centers for Disease Control and Prevention

THE NUMBER OF ALL CHILDREN HAS DROPPED

U.S. child population by age group in 2020, 2023, and 2028 (projected)

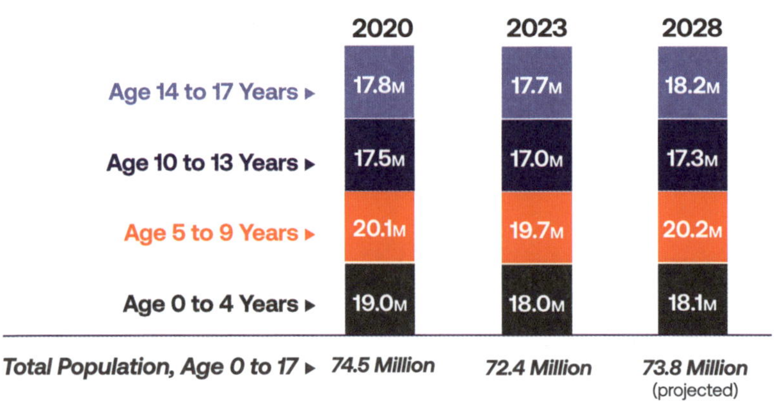

Source: NAIS Demographic Center

THE SCHOOL-AGE POPULATION HAS DROPPED IN MANY CITIES WITH MULTIPLE INDEPENDENT SCHOOLS

Change in population of children, 2020 to 2023

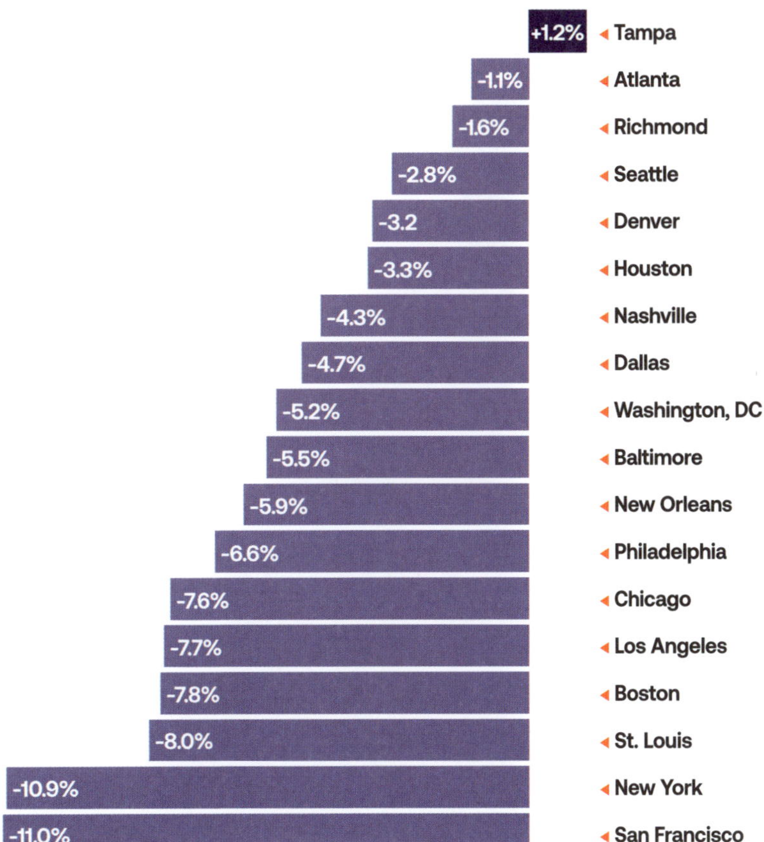

Source: NAIS Demographic Center

Enrollment

Current median enrollment at NAIS schools has surpassed pre-COVID levels. In 2023-2024, median enrollment achieved a 5% increase over 2019-2020. But growth varied widely by school type and location.

MEDIAN ENROLLMENT PER SCHOOL IS HIGHER THAN 2019-2020 LEVELS

Median total enrollment per school, 2019-2020 to 2023-2024

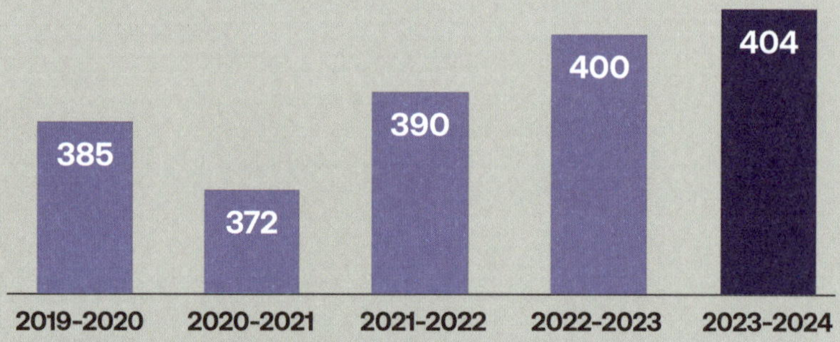

Source: NAIS, Data and Analysis for School Leadership (DASL)

ALMOST 2/3 OF SCHOOLS GREW SINCE 2019-2020

Change in median enrollment by school type, 2019-2020 to 2023-2024

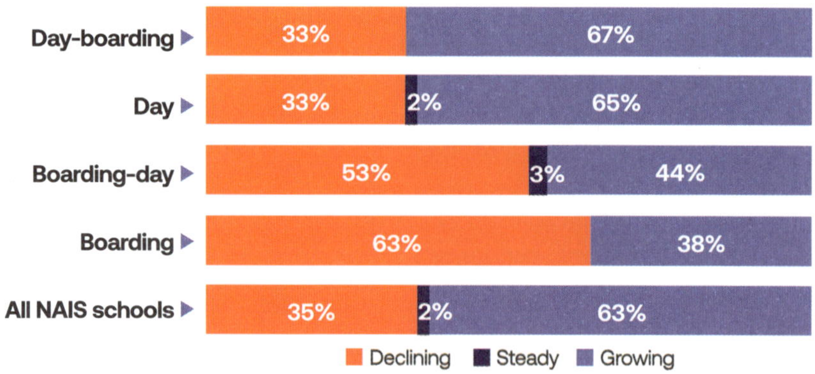

Source: NAIS, Data and Analysis for School Leadership (DASL)

Percentages in this Snapshot may not total 100% due to rounding.

MANY METRO AREAS WITH GROWING INDEPENDENT SCHOOL ENROLLMENT ARE IN THE SOUTHERN U.S.

Enrollment Change by Metro Area, 2019-2020 to 2023-2024

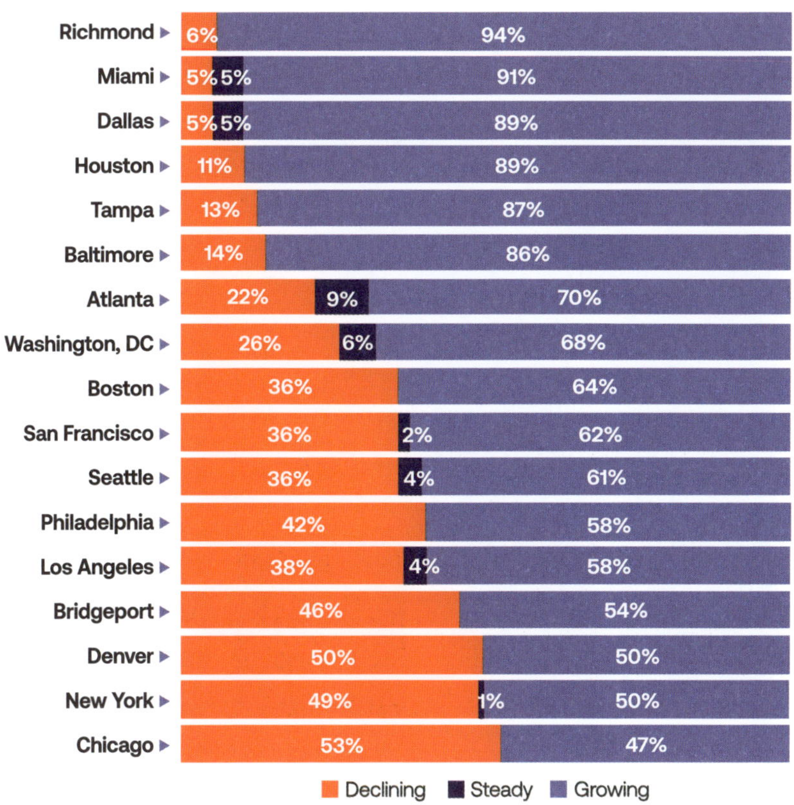

Source: NAIS, Data and Analysis for School Leadership (DASL)

Demand

Many NAIS schools are seeing positive signs in the admission funnel. As of 2022-2023, selectivity increased as median acceptance fell. Yield was up. Attrition was down.

NAIS SCHOOLS HAVE GROWN MORE SELECTIVE SINCE 2020-2021

Median acceptance rates at NAIS schools, 2018-2019 to 2022-2023

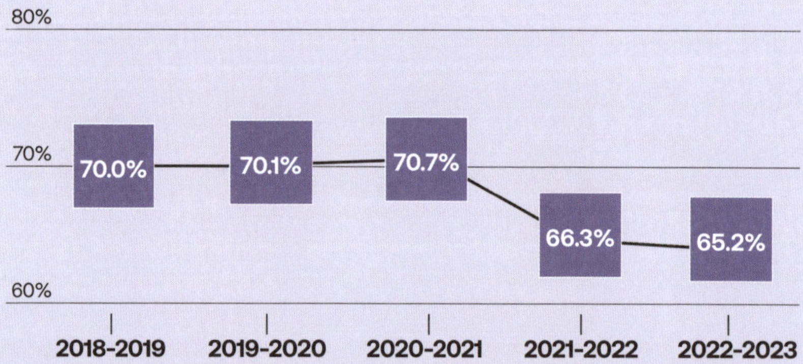

Source: NAIS, Data and Analysis for School Leadership (DASL)

SELECTIVITY VARIES BY SCHOOL TYPE

Median acceptance rates at NAIS schools, 2022-2023

Day schools	Day-boarding schools	Boarding-day schools	Boarding schools
66%	61%	59%	61%
2018-2019 median: 71%	*2018-2019 median: 65%*	*2018-2019 median: 57%*	*2018-2019 median: 59%*

Source: NAIS, Data and Analysis for School Leadership (DASL)

HIGHER YIELD RATES SIGNAL STRONGER DEMAND FOR INDEPENDENT SCHOOLS SINCE 2020-2021

Median yield rates at NAIS schools, 2018-2019 to 2022-2023

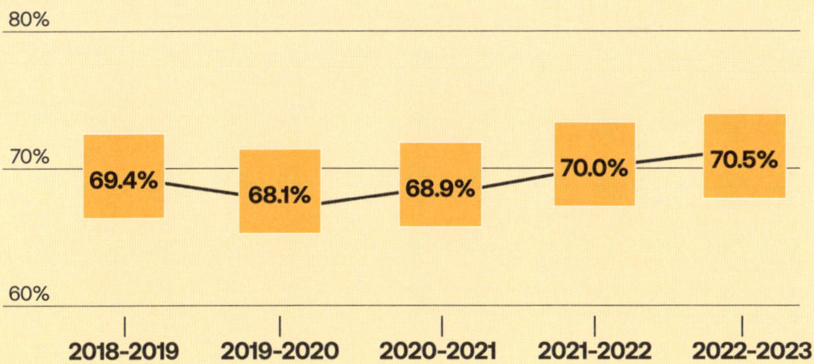

Source: NAIS, Data and Analysis for School Leadership (DASL)

DAY SCHOOLS HAD THE LOWEST ATTRITION IN 2022-2023

Median attrition rates by school type, 2022-2023

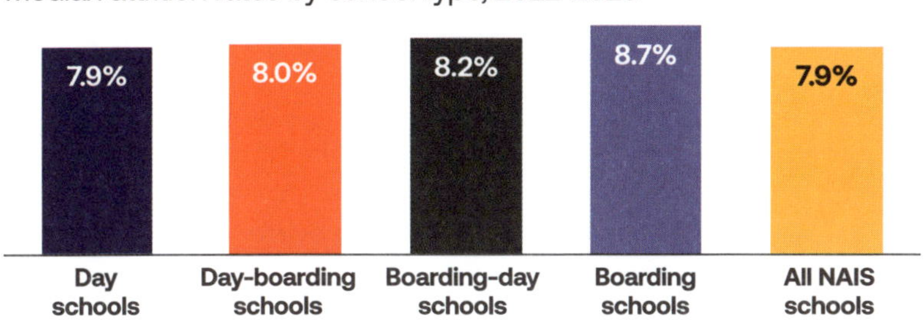

Source: NAIS, Data and Analysis for School Leadership (DASL)

Students

Independent schools' student populations are growing more diverse. The number of international students has rebounded slightly but is still down 26% since before the pandemic.

STUDENTS AT NAIS MEMBER SCHOOLS COME FROM DIVERSE BACKGROUNDS

Racial identities of students as a percentage of total enrollment

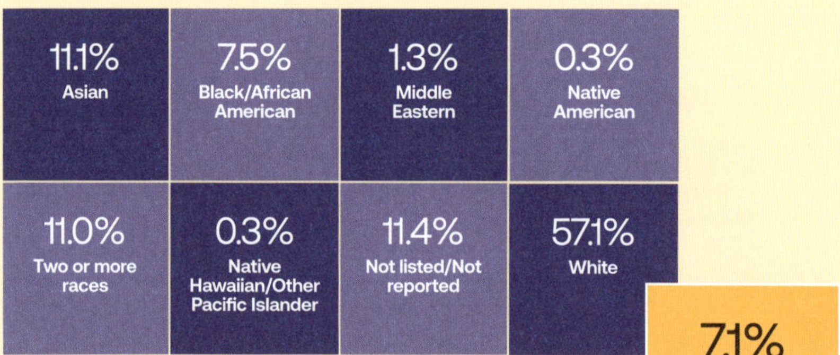

Sources: NAIS, Data and Analysis for School Leadership (DASL); percentages include domestic and international students

INDEPENDENT SCHOOLS HAVE SEEN A STEADY INCREASE IN STUDENTS OF COLOR

Students of color as a percentage of total domestic enrollment, 2019-2020 to 2023-2024

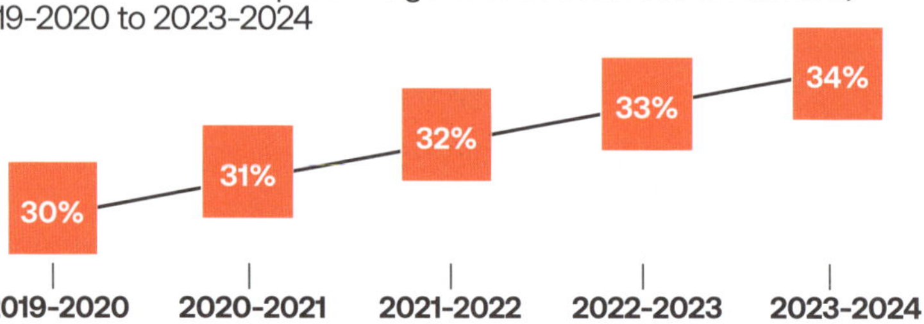

Source: NAIS, Data and Analysis for School Leadership (DASL)

THE NUMBER OF INTERNATIONAL STUDENTS IS UP, BUT STILL BELOW PRE-COVID LEVELS

Total international students on F-1 visas in NAIS member schools, 2019-2020 to 2023-2024

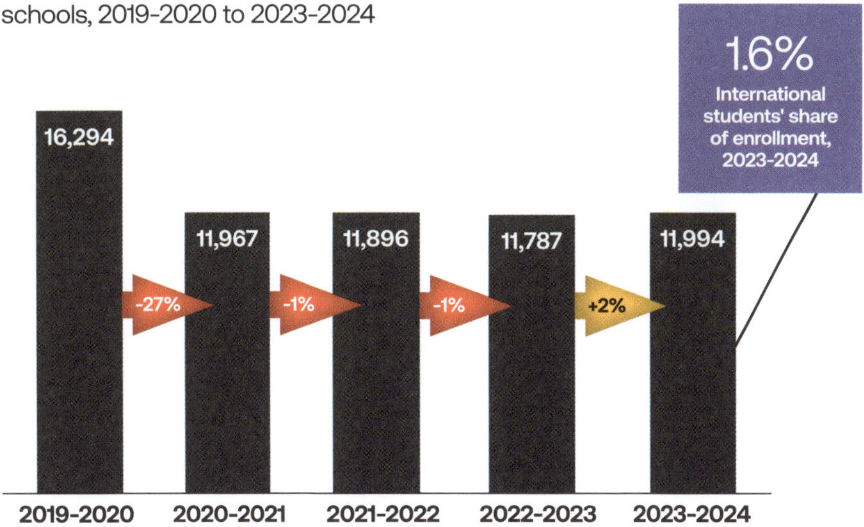

Source: NAIS, Data and Analysis for School Leadership (DASL)

TOP 5 SENDING COUNTRIES IN 2021-2022

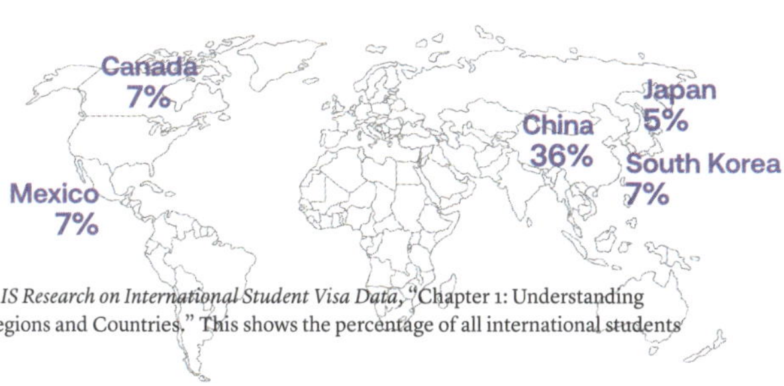

Source: Margaret Anne Rowe, *NAIS Research on International Student Visa Data*, "Chapter 1: Understanding International Student-Sending Regions and Countries." This shows the percentage of all international students originating from each country.

Finance

Independent schools' finances remain consistent, driven by net tuition and personnel costs. Despite an increase in 2023-2024, tuition still lags behind inflation. But financial aid has risen since 2019-2020.

THE VAST MAJORITY OF NAIS SCHOOLS' INCOME COMES FROM NET TUITION REVENUE

Percent of total revenue by category, 2022-2023

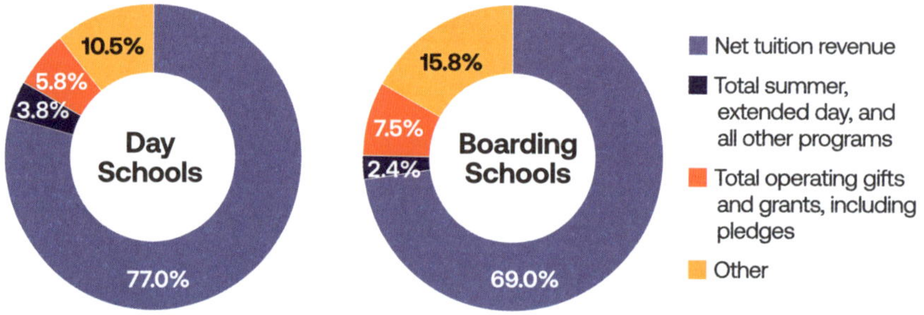

SALARIES AND BENEFITS MAKE UP MORE THAN HALF OF EXPENSES

Percent of total expenses by category, 2022-2023

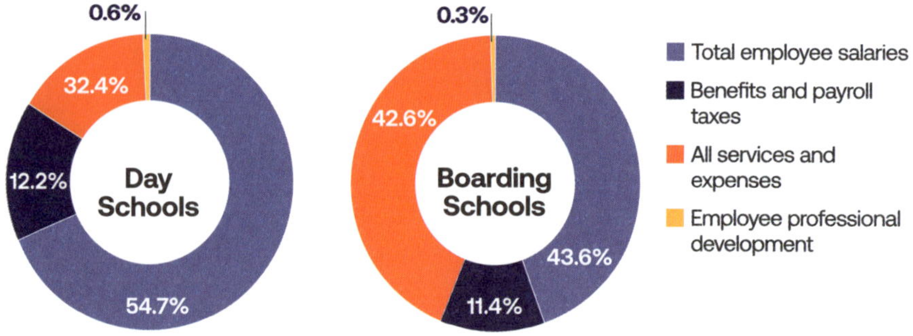

AS OF 2023-2024, INFLATION-ADJUSTED TUITION AND FEES WERE STILL BELOW PRE-PANDEMIC LEVELS

Median tuition and fees,* by student type, 2019-2020 and 2023-2024

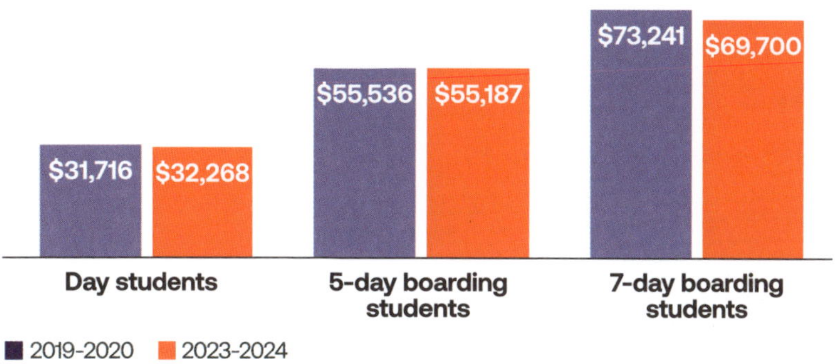

*Tuition and fees are calculated as the weighted average for grades 1 to 12.

MORE THAN 40% OF BOARDING STUDENTS AND NEARLY 25% OF DAY STUDENTS RECEIVED FINANCIAL AID IN 2023-2024

Percentage of students receiving financial aid by school type, 2023-2024

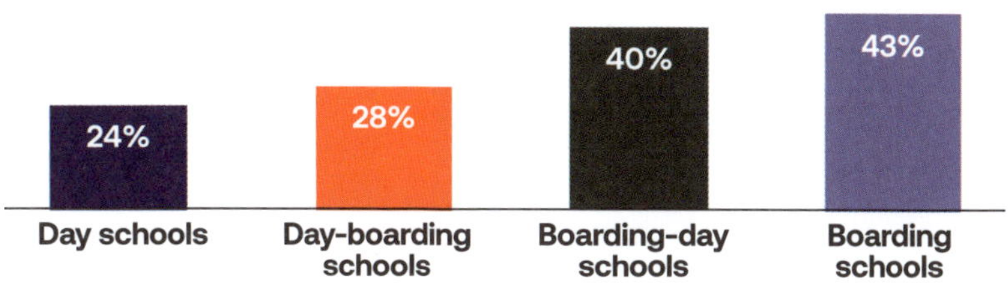

Source for all data: NAIS, Data and Analysis for School Leadership (DASL)

Percentages in this Snapshot may not total 100% due to rounding.

Philanthropy

Nationally, gifts to education are up. Independent schools are seeing varied giving patterns for different school types and donor groups.

GIVING USA REPORTS THAT DONATIONS TO ALL NONPROFITS FELL IN 2023. BUT THE EDUCATION SECTOR SAW GROWTH.

-2.1%
Total giving to nonprofits

+6.7%
Total giving to education

Source: Lilly Family School of Philanthropy, "Giving USA: U.S. Charitable Giving Totaled $557.16 Billion in 2023," June 2024. Percentages are inflation-adjusted.

THE PER-STUDENT AMOUNT NAIS SCHOOLS RAISED VARIED BY SCHOOL TYPE

Median average giving per student by school type, 2022-2023

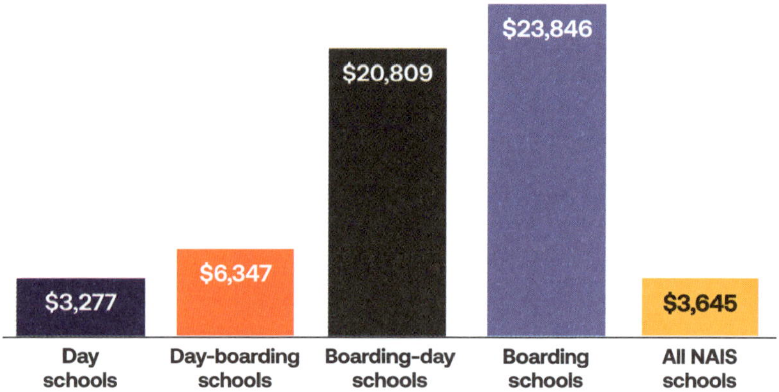

Source: NAIS, Data and Analysis for School Leadership (DASL)

DONOR PARTICIPATION HAS DECREASED SLIGHTLY AT INDEPENDENT SCHOOLS

Median participation rates by donor type at NAIS schools, 2021-2022 and 2022-2023

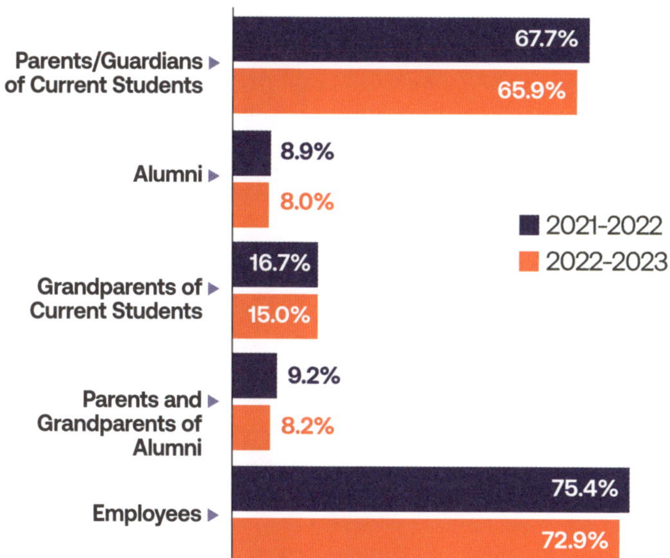

Source: NAIS, Data and Analysis for School Leadership (DASL)

MORE GIVERS USE DONOR-ADVISED FUNDS (DAFs) TO GIVE TO CHARITY

9%
Growth in contributions to DAFs between 2021 and 2022

29%
Portion of all DAF giving that goes to education

Sources: National Philanthropic Trust, "The 2023 DAF Report," and Philanthropy Roundtable, "Donor-Advised Funds: A Critical Lifeline for Education"

Leadership

The headship is growing more diverse, and rates of head transition are steady.

MORE WOMEN AND PEOPLE OF COLOR ARE SERVING AS SCHOOL HEADS

	% HEADS OF COLOR	% FEMALE HEADS
2013-2014	6.4	35.8
2018-2019	8.7	37.4
2023-2024	13.5	45.2

Source: NAIS, Data and Analysis for School Leadership (DASL)

THE HEAD TURNOVER RATE REMAINS STEADY DESPITE THE PANDEMIC

11%

Annual head turnover rate from 2019-2020 to 2022-2023

HOWEVER, THE AMOUNT OF UNEXPECTED TURNOVER HAS GROWN SLIGHTLY

24%

Heads who left their posts in 3 years or less. This number was 20% in 2018-2019.

AND HEADS AREN'T STAYING AS LONG AS THEY USED TO

7.3 years

Average tenure of sitting heads in 2023-2024. This number was 8.5 years in 2014-2015.

Source: NAIS internal data

Governance

The composition of independent school boards is shifting slowly, but many are staying the course logistically.

BOARD MAKEUP AND LOGISTICS

20

Average number of board members

This is up slightly from 19 members in 2018.

3 years

Typical board member term limit

20% of boards report no limit on renewable terms.

7

Average number of board meetings at a day school

Boarding schools average about 4 meetings per year.

BOARDS HAVE GROWN THEIR RACIAL AND GENDER DIVERSITY SINCE 2018

2018-2019		2023-2024
17%	TRUSTEES OF COLOR	24%
46%	FEMALE TRUSTEES	48%

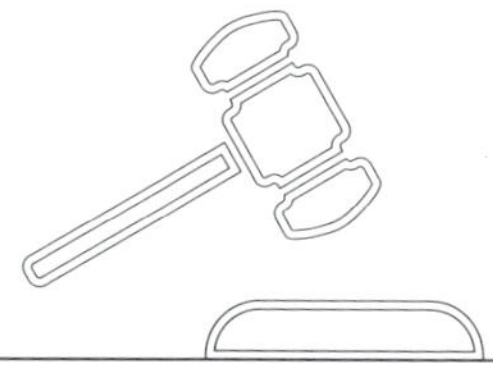

PARENTS AND PAST PARENTS MAKE UP MORE THAN 3/4 OF TRUSTEES ON THE AVERAGE BOARD

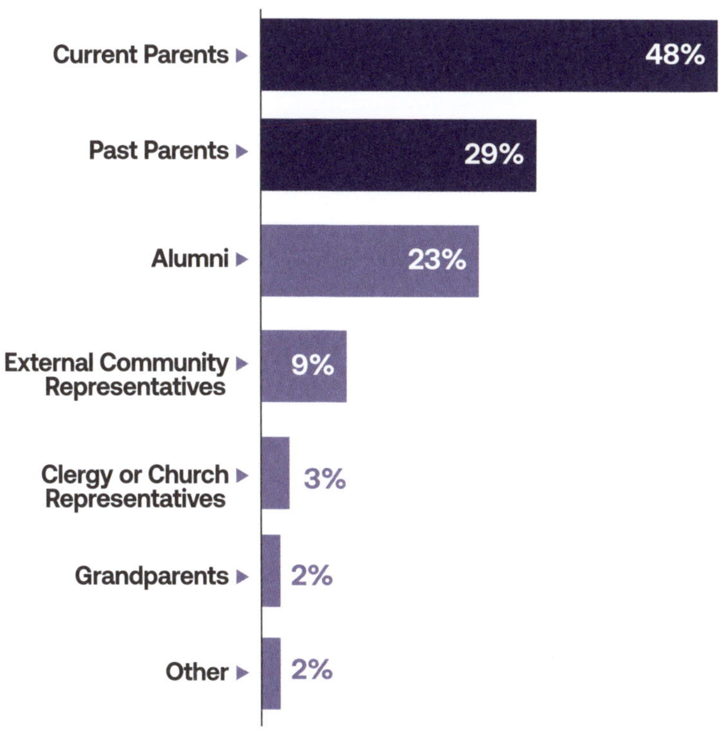

Total exceeds 100% because some board members fit in multiple categories.

Sources: All data in this Snapshot come from Margaret Anne Rowe and Amada Torres, *2023-2024 State of Independent School Governance, Part 1: Board Composition, Membership, Policies, and Practices*, except for the percentages of trustees of color, which come from NAIS, Data and Analysis for School Leadership (DASL).

EPILOGUE

Looking Forward

By Myra McGovern and Karla Taylor

Myra McGovern is vice president of external relations at NAIS.

Karla Taylor is the associate publisher.

The *2024-2025 NAIS Trendbook* synthesizes the latest trends and research to help you understand what's coming—because schools that are aware are better able to leverage opportunities and innovate for the future. In many ways, NAIS member schools are concrete manifestations of hope for the future. We are all committed to the children who will make tomorrow's world better than today's.

In this 15th edition, we pose probing questions to stimulate your thinking about a better future. As competition from alternative school types intensifies, what should your school do to convey its unique value for the price you ask? How might you use flexible workweeks and better professional development to recruit the best possible teachers? What does the expansion of private school choice programs mean for you?

And how should your school address student well-being? The world of artificial intelligence? The stress families feel as the college admission landscape continues to shift?

We hope that you will use this book as a springboard for discussions at board, administrative, and faculty meetings. We also hope that it spurs conversations within the independent school community about different approaches to issues and trends. In fall 2024, watch for NAIS webinars to help you put these and other trends in context and hear about other schools' experiences and solutions.

Independent schools have the freedom to innovate, creating exemplars for other schools. We see this diversity of approaches as a key asset for the NAIS community; we can all learn from each other to make the whole education system stronger. The unique missions and pedagogical approaches within the independent school community allow students to experience the education that works best for them.

As we chart the *Trendbook*'s future, we welcome feedback from you. Write to us at **trendbook@nais.org** with any comments and questions. Tell us how you plan to put this edition to work and which trends we should cover to help guide your future. That future—and the future of independent education—is of the utmost importance to us all.